Building with Logs

B. Allan Mackie

Charles Scribner's Sons
New York, New York

Building with Logs
©Canada, 1979, Seventh Edition
Log House Publishing Company Ltd.

1st published 1971, revised 1979 in Canada by
Log House Publishing Co.
of Prince George, British Columbia

Reprinted 1972, 1973, 1974, 1975, 1976, 1977, 1979, 1980

U.S. edition published by
Charles Scribner's Sons 1981

Copywritten under the
Berne Convention

1 3 5 7 9 11 13 15 17 19   I/C   20 18 16 14 12   10 8 6 4 2

Printed in Canada

Library of Congress Catalogue
Card Number 80-53966
ISBN Number 0-684-16959-2

Table of Contents

"...(Arthur Erickson) became more and more aware of historical tradition and increasingly began to distrust false inventiveness in new buildings and the use of new technological methods merely for the sake of technology. 'The past,' he notes, 'was responsible for some courageous buildings compared with the timidity of today'."

- p. 261, *Canadian Architecture 1960/1970.*

From the beginning
there have been
courageous log buildings
in Canada.

Samuel de Champlain's men
at Port Royal in 1605
used solid timber
and built magnificently. .

The Jesuits
at Midlands, 1639,
built the mission in solid timber
to a scale and exactitude
that astonished archaeologists
of the 20th century.

Hudson's Bay Company
heavy timber trading posts
throughout the West
still mark
the log building tradition.

John Moberly, HBC factor,
wrote in *When Fur Was King*
of substantial log houses
of the first settlers.

Many Canadians grew up in
log homes.

"...then rose the Log House
by the water side"
wrote Joseph Howe
in his poem, "Acadia", 1874.

And the census of 1821 found
⅔ of all Ontario homes
(28,571) were log.

Many of these Canadians
were famous,
and told about their homes,
or biographers
recorded how they were.

Laura Secord's father in 1795
built a log house
at Oxford Township, site of
the town of Ingersoll, Ontario.

Cedar logs
made the boyhood home
in Egypt, Ontario,
of Stephen Leacock.

"...beside
the curving trail
from Saint-Boniface

lay the family home...
plain, square-timbered,
with a steep-pitched roof...
for all its simplicity
a well-built little house",
the home of Louis Riel.

Nellie McClung
describes
all three of the family homes,
one in Ontario,
then, near Brandon, Manitoba
a quick one and, next winter, a
permanent home
all of "dressed timber
and whitewashed..."
In 1882 "we built our house:
logs
had been brought
for two winters
from the bush,
squared
and made ready...
and there came a great day
when the neighbours gathered
to raise the building.
A long table was set
in the shadow of the old house,
roast chicken, potatoes, turnips,
custard pie, currant buns,

and big pots of tea
cheered the workers...
That house was a great joy to us,
with a big room downstairs, a
bedroom for father and mother, a
large kitchen and pantry,
real stairs,
and two bedrooms above.
It still stands (1935),
a little bent
with the heaviness of years..."

There is
a W.L. Mackenzie King
log house
in Saskatchewan.

The largest log building
in the world is
at Montebello, Quebec.
An elegant C.P.R. hotel, it
was built in 1930
of British Columbia red cedar.

And to-day there are
three professional log
builder associations:
Western Canada,
Ontario and Quebec.

BUILDING WITH LOGS

in the 7th edition
is dedicated to those gallant Canadians who dare to continue this fine tradition of log building.

The axeman

in the twentieth century

displaying this determination

to find peace

and sanity

is joined in history

to every pioneer

who set himself to carving

a homestead

in a new world.

Many Canadians think of themselves as natural born axemen. Indeed, they are entitled to this image even though they may never have seen a tree felled, for it is still possible in this country to develop, with pride, these skills which were practised by our surprisingly recent ancestors.

This book was intended, originally, to encourage those Canadians who would leave the suburban reservations to live part of their lives at peace with nature. Over the years, this book has reached a far wider audience so that now, in its 7th edition, it is addressed to all those throughout the world who admire solid timber construction as one of the strongest, most durable and beautiful building forms known.

There are three prime reasons for using natural logs in construction. First, a log house is one of the most aesthetically satisfying in which to live. Logs bring the world of nature back into our lives in a way that becomes ever more necessary to our survival. There is a deep sense of peace, living in a house made of natural trees. No stripped, chipped, cooked, treated, compressed, or otherwise manufactured product of industrial technology can give such an awareness of each living tree, just as it once stood. You, as builder, will remember long after your house is finished, whether a tree had few limbs or many because of where it grew. You'll know how it looked as it fell to the ground. A scar may remind you of the day the logs were skidded to the building site. The length of time it took you to build will be recorded in the faint darkening of the rising logs as they became drier and less easy to peel. You will remember a log that chased you down the skids or one that humped its

back before it was subdued and fitted into place. The scrubbing, oiling, and perhaps varnishing will warm the colours and highlight the textures of the new walls ... revealing curves, limb lines, the lacework of bark beetles or the clawmarks of a bear ... all signs of nature to be saved and treasured. Finally, there is a growing understanding of all vegetation having consciousness. I accept that view. And I believe it accounts for that intense feeling of peace and thankfulness which permeates a natural, carefully-built log home. I leave it with the reader to consider what response the living spirit of a tree must feel when put to rest as part of your well-loved household.

The family that builds a log house knows their home as a work of art. They can savour it as no other. None but the log house provides its own sweet incense of sap and resin. Solid timber walls have an acoustic quality that makes music sound richer. Harsh household clatter does not strike, echo, and bounce as it does from plaster surfaces. The natural brown tones are restful to the eye. Above all, there is a quality of snug security in the fortress-thick walls. This may come from tradition, log construction being old and honoured in Canadian history. A log building ties that time tested tradition into our uncertain todays, giving a welcome sense of continuity and stability.

The second advantage of log construction is durability. With a good foundation to protect the wood from the composting urge of earth, and a wide overhang to shelter against rain and snow soakings, the log building will rival concrete in its long life. In style, the log house has an amazing durability. The pressures of fashion have never succeeded in making a log building look outdated. It is in timeless

good taste whether a simple building or the dramatic 20th century designs. Logs have an innate harmony with the landscape as long as they are used with dignity and with care.

Third: log construction is the only contemporary construction method which enables an individual to exchange labour and ingenuity, rather than cash or a mortgage indebtness, for a home to be proud of. Building with logs does require hard work; but it is healthy, pleasant work which is not at all beyond the strength of most families if it is undertaken at a pace that permits full appreciation of the undertaking as a once-in-a-lifetime experience. Our first home of only 700 square feet, on the shores of Francois Lake, was built in 1953 for a total cash outlay of two hundred dollars. The only purchased items were glass, roofing, spar varnish, and rough lumber. The rest was accomplished with a good deal of innovating, trading, scrounging, and neighbourly cooperation ... all activities which are still permissible in many parts of this country. But where the use of logs as building material requires not only the purchase and delivery of all materials but also the hiring of the builders, the log house will be as costly as frame or masonry construction. This should not deter the family able to afford what pleases them most. And savings will occur both in heating and airconditioning as well as in the low cost of building maintenance over the centuries.

So let us begin the discussion of how to build with logs knowing this to be a discussion, for there are always different ways to do each task. Every axeman will find many new answers of his own. This is part of the craft. It is what helps to make each house unique ... a work of art.

The tree, as building material

I am going to ask that this discussion on log building construction begin with a close look at the tree as it stands in nature, before a hand is laid upon it. Many of us have two hang-ups about trees: agrarian and cultural. In the agrarian past, the tree was an enemy. It constantly threatened to invade pastures and fields or it was already using land which could otherwise provide food crops. The farmer waged a constant war to eradicate trees from his holdings and, in the past, it was more of an equal battle. But with the coming of the bulldozer, farmers gained the upper hand. Never again would he need to fear that the forest would reclaim his land. The agrarian instinct was not calmed, however. People rushed headlong about the landscape fighting the war against nature, toppling trees and heaping them up for burning just as rubbish is burned. The joy of victory carried us ever onward, clearing and breaking much forest land which should never have been expected to grow anything else but timber. The ancestral urge for land is not an easy instinct to curb. And often I wonder if this urge resurfaces in the urbanized setting as an unthinking contempt for trees, as of yore. But that's only one hang-up. The other I've called cultural for industrial sales have helped reshape our values away from natural shapes and textures and toward an appreciation of a "finished" product. We've learned to distrust the possibility that one of life's necessities could be found perfect in nature. Food, one might suppose, grows in supermarkets. And then they began to wax the turnips, thinking they'd look better when they appeared in the store. And so, with this same mixed training in realism, some people approach the building of a log house feeling that the tree, as it is found in nature, is not quite good enough; that it should have (as a longtime logger said to me) "some kind of finish".

A close look at the tree's physical properties will help overcome both these hang-ups. First, the body of the tree is composed of hollow cells, either tube-like or brick-shaped, packed closely together. Under a microscope, they look like a honeycomb. When the tree is felled and the vital fuilds have dried, these tiny air pockets seal, becoming a most perfectly insulated building material. This explains why a log house remains so cool during the summer and why it takes so many days to chill off if left during the winter. It also explains why sounds are absorbed and why music floats so softly through the rooms of a solid timber building. Vapour control is taken care of, too; household moisture is not absorbed to any degree by the log and yet, any which does exist internally will find its own route out as it always did, via the log ends.

Therefore, the tree as it exists naturally is already an almost perfect building material. And for "finish", if the bark has been peeled with care so that no gouging, scarring, or scratching of the wood is allowed to occur, the log will dry to the sort of satiny finish that tempts hands to reach out and stroke it. Do so, for that's how to fully appreciate its smoothness. If, next, the log is washed free of dirt, allowed to dry again, and given a single oiling with boiled linseed oil or Danish oil, the surface becomes not only satin-

smooth but also sufficiently waterproof on the inside to resist household vapour. I know of no sawn, cut, or "finished" wood of any kind, as capable of this--and it is my opinion that a tree is the product of millions of years of tree trial, proven successful. It only remains for us as builders to accord the tree the respect it deserves.

The tree, as an endangered species

It is also good to keep in mind, as we approach the study of solid timber construction, that the log builder is in an enviable position of being able to preserve a part of the relentless harvest of an endangered species.

Under to-day's export-oriented trading conditions, the tree is doomed. Like the buffalo, the trumpeter swan, the sea otter, and the whole sweet-natured legion of beings who have brought swift and easy profits to people who never cared that such bounty might end, the tree simply cannot grow fast enough or reproduce swiftly enough to survive the toll being taken of them.

It requires at least 100 years to grow a mature tree and up to 500 years for it to reach its maximum growth as shown in the following photos from the British Columbia Archives. The best forest technology can only speed that process up to a 50-year period. But in the meantime, economic pressures are forcing the logging industry into an almost irresistible trend toward harvesting younger timber, especially if it is close to any road. Industry cannot be held fully at fault, for it is the general public which cries out for

Right: 1895, near Vancouver, British Columbia, this Douglas Fir stood 417 feet tall with 300 feet to its first limbs; circumference at base: 77 feet; butt diameter: 25 feet.

Lower, centre: *Douglas Fir circa 1900.*

Lower left and lower right: Western Red Cedar.

"employment" and the government must ask industry to set up the conditions for mass employment. Enormous cash profits are needed to establish mills, factories, and the supporting cities. There is little alternative, in such circumstances, but to mow the trees down as if the forests were fields of ripe wheat. And, afterwards, to search out any customer or create any product geared to immediate cash sales. Thus, it might not be entirely tragic if the giant timbers were gone but something splendid remained in their place. But instead we get smouldering moonscapes of stumps and subsoil, because every tree was either trampled or needed to pay the unbelievable costs of the tree shears, forwarders, skidders, loaders, and logging trucks which haul them to the mills. And instead of noble architecture or even a well-housed population, we're more likely to get toilet tissue, newsprint, paper towelling, advertising flyers, fake wallboard, and cardboard cartons . . . and next day, much of that is in the rivers, heaped in land-dumps, or smouldering into the atmosphere. National economic policies which try single-mindedly to create jobs are often bogged down in the notion that the more processes a natural resource is subjected to, the more employment it creates, with greater advantage to all. But higher costs plus less real productivity equals the formula for inflation: less purchasing capability for the ones who need those jobs. Thus many people cannot afford to buy, from their earnings in the industrial workplace, the products they manufacture. Some opt for debt; others choose to build with natural, usually free, materials, such as logs. Those who treasure what timber we still have, are the Conservers, building for tomorrow. There is employment aplenty

in this option, as every good 20th century log builder knows. These careful builders may yet write the mighty chapter in Canadian architectural history showing how rare and beautiful logs naturally are, as building material.

Not only is the tree slow-growing, it is also painfully slow to reproduce. It isn't at all like the herbs which can reach maturity and cast seed in one summer — it requires many years of undisturbed growth before the first cones can provide seed. Tree-planting might be argued, as a solution to sustaining the forests but there are many hazards working against it as a completely successful practice. And further, tree-planting lags far behind tree-harvesting. John Walters, director of the University of British Columbia's research forest operations, calls it "The Great Forest Rip-Off" in the December/January 1974 issue of Big Wheel Logging News: "500,000 acres logged per year and 250,000 acres burned per year but only 110,000 acres planted per year!" That's in British Columbia where ½ the provincial budget comes from timber revenues.

Trees have no adequate defence against human encroachment: land-clearing and farming, erosion, chemicals, fires. They have absolutely no defense against highway systems, industrial complexes, power developments, airports, stripmining, and all the housing and blacktopping and shopping-plaza forms of urbinization. But above all, trees cannot possibly continue to exist when these massive profits are needed to support what we call "employment" and when these trees are the raw ingredient upon which the mills, factories, and cities are feeding.

It is important to know that the tree, under these circumstances, is doomed. To build correctly, the log builder must be aware that he still has the priceless opportunity to preserve some trees as architecture. In so doing he will be creating something of perhaps greater longterm social value that he may, at first, appreciate. Certainly I never as fully understood this fact myself as I did when visiting the Grey Nuns' House (shown next) at Saint-Boniface and the Curator explained to me that this four storey building had been hewn of oak. Oak! I could scarcely believe that such timbers had ever existed. But there they were, almost as beautiful after 130 years of seasoning in those walls, as they must have been as trees growing along the banks of the Red River. It was at that moment, I fully realized that the log builder acts as custodian, preserving the best of the logs from an era. Good log buildings may, in the next century, be all that's left of our vanished forests. The Grey Nuns' House is certainly one of the few fragments the nation has left of those oaks that once grew . . . and may never be seen again . . . on the Red River in Manitoba.

"I wish all to know that I do not propose to sell any part of my country, nor will I have the whites cutting our timber along the rivers, more especially the oak. I am particularly fond of the little groves of oak trees. I love to look at them, because they endure the wintry storm and the summer's heat, and — not unlike ourselves — seem to flourish by them."

— Chief Sitting Bull (Tatanka Yotanka)

Interior wall of hewn oak, Grey Nuns' House.

Three conservation practices for the log builder

Leaving aside corporate and industrial problem-solving, three methods of forest conservation are of special concern to the log builder. Under the broad general aim of making optimum use of timber resources, he should be particularly aware of (1) how he logs ... (2) how he builds ... (3) what he builds.

The log builder is fortunate if he can go into the woods to pick out the trees he'll be working with. This way he obtains the size and the conformity of log he prefers. He also gets the trees out undamaged and a fine set of building logs not gouged, scraped, shattered, or scarred by machinery is a great beginning for a house. Most important, however, is the opportunity of leaving an undisturbed forest able, within only a few years more, to provide its next crop. Selective logging makes this possible. Loggers familiar with selective logging methods believe it to be the most profitible and efficient way of sustaining the supply of

timber over the longterm, despite the fact that it appears to be the slowest. I know of forests where major logging had been undertaken, over the same terrain, every 10 years . . . until the big yellow machines moved in and mowed everything down in the clearcut method which, in my opinion, requires a minimum of 100 years to recuperate. Or as one old logger said, more realistically, "Let's face it, it's gone forever. Nobody will log here again."

Consider another example of making the optimum use of timber: one logging truckload of logs can sustain only a few hours' activity in the mill or plywood plant . . . but a truckload of good logs can provide a year's highly paid work for the log builder who, furthermore, creates a product of far higher market value. And without soil pollution, air pollution, or water pollution. Most of the income goes to the men doing the work rather that to pay for machinery. What's more, the log builder didn't need a foreign investor to set him up in an industrial complex or government to supply him with a city or urban services. He initiates secondary work for those who make blacksmith's hardware or leaded glass windows, as well as for carvers and stonemasons, and for the plumbers, electricians, floor layers, and so on. The log builder is in a privileged position, really: a free man, handsomely paid, engaged in healthful work, valued in the community.

But any privilege, to endure, must be based in social responsibility. An intelligent society will not long tolerate the man who tries to cream off truck loads of resources for questionable use. Therefore, *how he builds* is of special concern. If the ancient and honoured craft is to survive he'll shape and fit logs

The room of "The Order of Good Cheer" as it was in 1605. Note size of knee braces.

Roof trussing as built by ships' carpenters in Champlain's "Habitation", Port Royal, Nova Scotia.

France not only encouraged excellent builders but also took care to preserve their architectural drawings, thus making it possible to rebuild in exact detail such significant structures as Champlain's "Habitation" (shown above) just as it was in 1605, Port Royal, as well as part of the Fortress of Louisbourg, 1720-45.

trades, and doing all of this under modern conditions, by all the urban and suburban rules, yet he's still working hand-in-glove with nature in a non-polluting, humanistic way. He is one of the real trail-blazers of the future . . . if he holds true to his own beliefs and methods, and especially to his own colleagues.

Therefore, *what he builds,* can be safely assumed in these 1980 s, will be nothing but strong, handsome log buildings. But let me tell you: this safe assumption was hard-won. It represents a most significant milestone in the developmental sequence of the modern log building renaissance.

The Lawg Caybun concept in building

When BUILDING WITH LOGS was first written, early in 1971, the word "cabin" appeared nowhere in it. Certainly, I was aware that log cabins existed, both literally and linguistically. But as I myself did not use the term and did not live in, build, or teach about cabins, it was my uncomplicated belief that the term had nothing to do with me or my book. It was an error of omission. For several years, my students and I endured that double-edged sword: praise for my log cabins, compliments on my log cabin book. The more I ignored it, the more the term seemed to thrive . . . like a weed unplucked. So the 4th, 5th, and 6th editions addressed the question. I showed how the term had originated and why the term had come to have less of its original meaning as shelter for the poor, the oppressed, or the actual slaves . . . and to have more and more meaning as an exalted political symbol of possible upward social mobility.

as tightly as ever ships' timbers were fitted. His artistic judgment will put fine logs to their finest use, as did Champlain's carpenters. He'll meet or exceed every aspect of any national building code. Let the log builder view this high standard of work as straight economic dollars and sense. Or let him build beautifully as an act of faith in the future, or of homage to the past. Whatever his motivation, the front-rank log builder knows that the road to excellence is the only way to go if we

are to safeguard this great privilege of building with logs. If we succeed in combining productivity with elegance and excellence, society sees that it's good business, working with nature. If we fail, it helps convince society that mills and factories can do everything better. In my opionion, a great responsibility rests upon the 20th century log builder . . . for he's one of the rare industries working to full employment, creating a valuable product, employing many secondary spin-off

Profil et Elevation du batiment a faire en Charpente pour le Logement du Lieutenant du Roy 1733

French military engineers and draftsmen were one of the most skilled professional classes of the time. Plans they produced routinely were carefully drawn and coloured and are characterized by their meticulous detail as well as artistic embellishment. It is not generally recognized how much we owe to the French engineers for our visual record of Louisbourg, and much of North America. The drawings made throughout New France show how common was this technical expertise and how often it resulted in a superlative record of buildings. . .

Louisbourg was large enough to have commercial, military, residential districts . . . public buildings were monumental . . . Where else in the North American colonies during that period (early 1700's) were structures comparable in size and concept to the Casernes of Louisbourg or the Artillery Barracks in Quebec City . . .? Did any activity elsewhere result in a body of maps and plans comparable to those created by the French?

- Bulletin of the Assoc. Preservation Technol. Vol. IV, #1-2, 1972.

The Lartigue house being rebuilt to look as it did in 1735 when it belonged to the Fortress of Louisbourg, Cape Breton Island.

Right: 1735 houseplans for a similar home

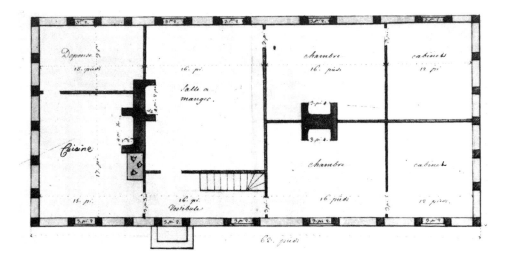

Log builders laugh now, when they recall the old battles waged and won. It took a while. A great many people wrote and I especially appreciated those letters from the U.S.A. thanking me for making the difference clear, between the politics and the building concept, and saying they saw improved results just from that new understanding.

So in these enlightened times, few people mistake a house for a cabin. They know that we are not cabin-builders. Just to be on the safe side, and for those who did not see the previous editions, it may be prudent to go over the main arguments against that cabin concept.

My premise was that the term, "log cabin", had done greater injury to the proper development of log buildings than had all the bark beetles, termites, dry rot, lightening strikes, mildew, uncaring tenants, or bad workmanship in all history.

The log cabin term has no legitimate place in Canadian history. The French from earliest Champlain (Port Royal, 1605) used logs magnificently. The British also held a firm conviction in maintaining the timber framing techniques they had always known. And even when such groups as the United Empire Loyalists arrived from the United States as refugees, they quickly contrived shelters of log which they then called "shanties" or "huts" but never "cabins" . . . they knew too well its slave connotation. Later when they built a family home, usually of log, it was called a house. Naturally. Shown above is a typically neat hewn log home of 19th century Ontario. It is the kind of home to which settlers often brought, at great pains, at least one object of great beauty: a piano, a set of fine

china, a carved bed . . . to which they pointed with pride, hoping for the day when they could furnish their entire household to that standard. The above home succeeded in doing that.

I had found, too, that the cabin concept was crippling for students who could not be unlocked from the grip of that stereotype. Those who imagined log building construction to be a survey of rustic, rough shelters had destroyed most of their opportunity to learn how to build well. Good concept is the prerequisite for a builder. It defines any project.

One of the most dramatic log homes built by any of my students was done by an English teacher and his Librarian wife, neither of whom had had any previous building experience of any sort. But they did have intelligence, stamina, ambition, and above all a tremendous appreciation

of what solid timber could be made to do. They could relate whatever they heard, saw, or practised in class to this expanded concept. As a result, their home has impact. To enter its main hall is to stop, struck by the many expressions of openness, height, light, warmth, colours, spatial arrangements, and much more which is difficult to articulate . . . something very much to do with the richness of the human heritage, timeless and undaunted just so long as it is valued.

Finally to illustrate further the power of good concept, I described the lady who willingly did enough homework in 1972 for me to realize fully the consequences of a log cabin stereotype. She asked my advice: would two fireplaces (and no furnace) provide adequate heat throughout a Prairie winter in the 61 ft. by 44 ft. "log cabin" she and her husband proposed to build. It was an important point, she explained, because they hoped to raise a family and live forever in that 2,684 square foot dream home but wanted it to be "as authentic as possible", i.e., no heat. She intended sawing barrels in half to serve as appropriate living room furniture and thanked me for my efforts "to bring this lifestyle back into existence". I couldn't imagine what she meant . . . but suspected the Lawg Caybun stereotype was at work degrading her blueprint and threatening to render her home "authentic-awful". The best help I thought I could give her was remedial reading. She was a good student. "No, I didn't notice that you never used the word 'cabin' anywhere in your book," replied a

somewhat subdued correspondent. "I did as you instructed and looked the word up in a dictionary. It in no way describes the structure in which we plan to live. It is also true that I would never have referred to it as a 'cabin' had we been planning to build a brick or plywood structure. In fact, since you pointed out its meaning, I have formed a passionate dislike for the word . . ." She needed no other help than this change of concept. With the image corrected, she was easily able to make the necessary heating improvements to her houseplan as well as to upgrade the interior furnishings to chairs more appropriate to a permanent residence of that scope and significance. The lesson left me indebted, however, for it was the first time I saw clearly illustrated the devastating influence of Lawg Caybunism, thanks to her patient study. And it was this lady who brought to my attention the way in which Shakespeare had used the word "cabin" to mean unhappy confinement, as in MacBeth:

"But now I am Cabin'd, cribb'd, confin'd,
    bound in to saucy doubts and fears . . ."

That pioneers of bygone centuries wasted timber on some small, bad buildings is undeniable. But they worked to survive, the trees were being felled and burned to create fields, and, besides, they knew no better. We do . . . and so logs, in this day and age, ought to be the unthinkable material for "cabin"-making. Let there be an end to the travesty of mimicking the worst that pioneers did while ignoring their best. I am especially sad when conservationists and wilderness buffs, those pollution-fighting resource-protecting outdoors people, are to be found leading the parade of "cabin"-lovers. I agree, there is a special joy in the

wilderness camp, the summer cottage, the mountain lookout . . . but these temporary, substandard structures are unworthy of solid timber construction. Rather, let the conservationists be the first to pitch tents or to build with plywood, insisting that those 40 or 50 trees be left to grow until someone can carefully craft them into centuries-enduring buildings.

The log builder is enjoying what could be the dying hours of a privileged profession, if care is not taken. If society is to allow him -- and perhaps even to encourage him -- to continue working in a medium so fast disappearing from even our most favoured regions, the log builder must lead the way in woods conservation. Let us resolve, therefore, to take sufficient time to log selectively wherever possible . . . to work carefully . .

and to produce log buildings of the highest order of beauty and excellence. It can be no other way, if we hope to continue building with logs.

Tools

The tie hackers and shake splitters who moved into the bush to work the winter, not so very many years ago, were said to have had their sawmills on their backs. This was true, inasmuch as they could build their own accommodation for the winter with the tools they could carry: a double-bitted axe, a broad axe, a crosscut saw or framesaw, an auger bit (the handle to made in the woods), plus a piece of sheet metal for the stove and a small packet of shingle nails. This, along with a bedroll and a few days' supply of groceries, set a man up in business.

Conditions in the woods have changed greatly . . . for loggers. But for the lone woodsman, the basic tools -- with the exception of the chain saw -- have changed little. Because your building is going to be larger and of a more permanent nature, there is need for a somewhat expanded list of tools. The most important of these, in addition to a basic set of carpenter's tools, is a log scriber, a peeling spud, and log dogs.

A pair of good scribers is essential, for these are the key to measuring for perfectly fitted logs. Their helpfulness cannot be overestimated.

Many types and designs of scribers have been made, generally by the person who expects to use them. So, purely as a guide, I have included in a later section of this book when we come to walls and the actual use of the scriber, a dimensioned diagram of the ones which I have found to be most successful. My favourite ones were made from an old chain saw blade. But scribers can also be made from a heavy pair of machinist's or tinsmith's dividers and I also use a pair like this, fitted up with a level which is custom-made for the Mackie School. By means of this level, it is possible to see at all times whether or not the instrument is being held in the correct perpendicular position. For marking, they are fitted with an indelible pencil which puts a clear mark on any log, green, wet, or dry.

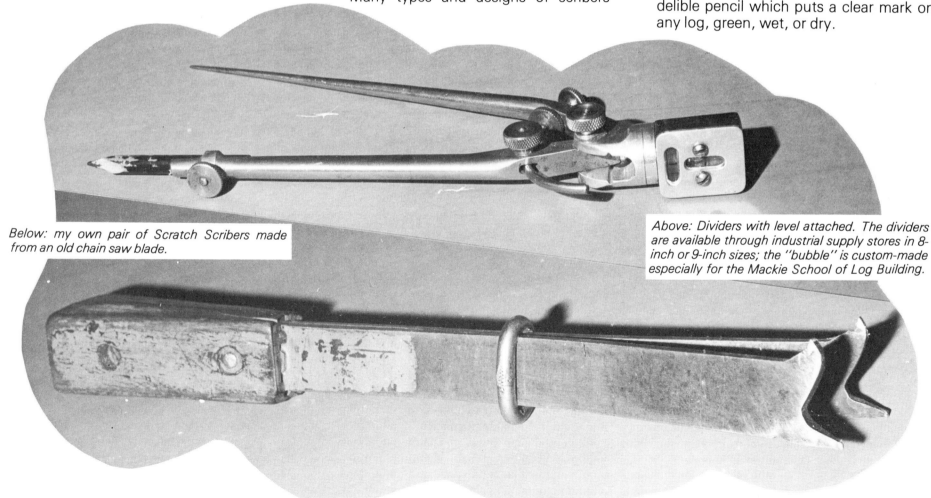

Below: my own pair of Scratch Scribers made from an old chain saw blade.

Above: Dividers with level attached. The dividers are available through industrial supply stores in 8-inch or 9-inch sizes; the ''bubble'' is custom-made especially for the Mackie School of Log Building.

Scribers should be strong enough to be able to cut or mark a good clear line in the log. They must also be handy enough to fit close to the log on the corners. They should have a way to set the distance between the points firmly, without danger of slipping. "Fin" type scribers can be made by a blacksmith and very good ones of this kind can be made from a No. 4 coyote trap, which has the added advantage of keeping the trap from being any further danger to the coyotes. Cut the eyes of the spring through at right angles to the spring so that they have a fishtail cutting edge. Heat and squeeze the spring to a sharper bend and put a keeper around it. In use, the cutting points are set at the desired distance with a small block of wood and then the keeper is driven up tightly.

LOG DOGS

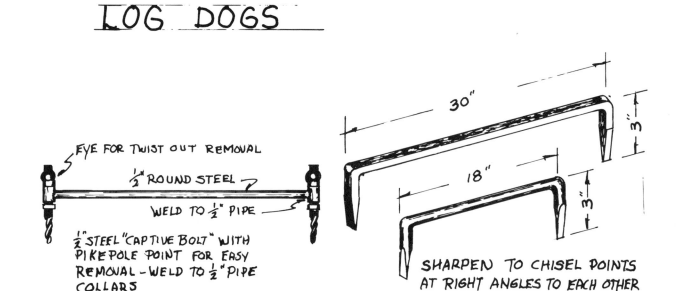

EYE FOR TWIST OUT REMOVAL

½" ROUND STEEL

WELD TO ½" PIPE

½" STEEL "CAPTIVE BOLT" WITH PIKE POLE POINT FOR EASY REMOVAL—WELD TO ½" PIPE COLLARS

30"

18"

3"

3"

SHARPEN TO CHISEL POINTS AT RIGHT ANGLES TO EACH OTHER

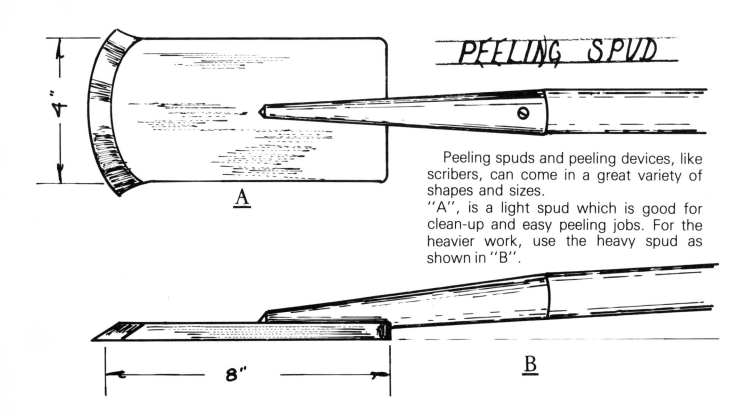

PEELING SPUD

4"

A

8"

B

Peeling spuds and peeling devices, like scribers, can come in a great variety of shapes and sizes.

"A", is a light spud which is good for clean-up and easy peeling jobs. For the heavier work, use the heavy spud as shown in "B".

Log dogs can be made from ¾" square steel, about 36" long. Sharpen each end to a chisel point and bend about 3" of each end down. These, when driven into the building at one end, and into the log on which you are working at the other end, will hold the log firmly in place. A smaller pair of log dogs, about 12 or 14" long, can also be very handy.

The tool that can accomplish a great deal in a short time is a gasoline-powered chain saw. Because it is noisy and smoky is not enough to recommend that a good axe be used in its place, but experience has indicated that the chain saw is perhaps even more dangerous than was

originally understood. In addition to the immediate dangers of coming in contact with the chain, there is increasing evidence that high vibration levels are causing serious circulatory problems. Vibratory White Finger, or Raynaud's Disease, is the occupational hazard to be feared by all who hold a vibrating tool in their hands, be that a pneumatic drill, a shoe repair lathe, or a chain saw. It is far more widespread than one, at first, might imagine. This, in part, is due to the fact that the initial symptoms appear so trivial: a slight tingling in the finger tips, followed later by a numbness, then by a distinctive white colour which is the sure danger signal that the blood supply has been temporarily cut off. If exposure continues, the damage continues until the fingers cannot be made to button up clothing or pick up small objects. Unless the operator stops using the vibrating tool, the final result is gangrene for which the only cure is amputation. Another chain saw related occupational hazard is loosely termed "sawdust asthma" caused by the extremely fine sawdust particles from dry or treated wood. Breathing this - in my own case, for even 5-minute periods, now -- brings on this bronchial disorder. At the end of 1977, when I had taught 15 short courses from the University of British Columbia's Pacific shores, to Seafoam County, Nova Scotia, I was coughing blood at the end of some lectures. It was two years before I was willing to risk this level of exposure again . . . and I am doing some Eastern seaboard teaching, now, with the aid of an assistant. My work at the Mackie School of Log Building is similarly curtailed to lectures and specific demonstrations. I have found the simple cure for both these serious occupational hazards: the axe. I

use an axe, now, as much as possible.

I don't really favour one brand of saw above another because almost any saw gives good service if it is looked after

correctly. But, in general, a very big saw is too dangerous to handle in high or awkward places on a building, and the itty bitty saws developed for Cheechakos are, in spite of the manufacturers' claims, usually good for nothing. Use a moderate size saw of 4 to 4.5 cubic inch displacement and with a relatively high cutting speed. Bar length should be 16 to 20 inches. The shorter bar is good for working on the building but the longer bar is needed for falling trees. Some saws have a high noise characteristic and, out of respect for your eardrums, should be avoided. And, of course, you'll be looking for vibration-damping characteristics in any saw you buy, plus the absolutely essential Chain Brake which stops the action instantly in case of kickback. As some protection against ear and eye damage, I recommend the wearing of a crash helmet with full plastic screen covering the face. There are padded gloves on the market, too, which help a little in protecting the hands from White Finger disease.

To look after a chain saw, observe two rules: mix the gasoline and oil properly; and keep the chain sharp, properly tensioned and well oiled. The manufacturer will recommend a mixing proportion of gasoline and oil for the particular saw . . . this may be 16 parts gasoline to one part oil, or it may be as high as 50 parts gasoline to one part oil. The use of synthetic oils will again affect this ratio.

Whatever the mix, pour a portion of the carefully measured original volume back into a smaller container. Add the oil to this smaller amount. And mix throroughly. When mixing is complete, pour this mix back into the larger amount and stir again. If some oil remains in the small container, which may happen in cold weather, pour some of the mix back again until all the oil is suspended in the gasoline. When pouring the mix into the gasoline tank of the saw, use a strainer funnel and be careful to avoid having sawdust or snow enter the tank.

Chain filing and tensioning are best done in accordance with the manufacturer's recommendation for the saw. I prefer to file the teeth at a lesser horizontal angle than is generally used for bucking logs. I reduce this angle to 25°

instead of the usual 35° . . . this causes the saw to cut slower, but it will produce a smoother cut on a notch and the chain will rip faster when doing a lateral groove.

POOR   DOUBTFUL   GOOD

Choose an axe handle with a good clean edge grain, as at right above.

Axes are, to a large extent, a matter of personal preference. I no longer use the double-bitted axes because they have proven too dangerous where there are several people around a work-site. A number of good axes have come onto the market since the demand has increased so dramatically in the last several years. These are the 4 to 5½ lb. axes with excellent finish and balance. Good handles are also available, if one is careful enough in selection. Choose a 28" to 30" handle that has a good clean edge grain, is made of hickory without sap wood, and of course is straight.

Axes should be kept sharp. File into the bit, "cutting" the file with the axe. A good handle on the file prevents cuts if the file slips. Start filing a distance back from the edge and work out to the edge. This will keep the blade slim and parabolic in shape. Too thin an edge will chip or bend, but an axe must be sharp, as a dull axe can slip or glance off the wood.

The owner of a good 2-inch auger is lucky for this is not an easy tool to find. The only care it nees is protection of the edges from gravel, dirt, or nails. Grease it well before storage to prevent rust. In use, a hand auger should not be expected to bore through more than one log at a time. . .unless it is very long, it will jam up with chips and, once taken out of the cut, it is hard to start again. Bridge augers will drill deeper, particularly if power driven.

Holes may also be cut with a gouge type of chisel. This chisel has a long curved blade and is sharpened on the inside. It should have a heavy shank so it may be driven with a hammer. I first saw this type of drill among the tools used for making Red River carts, shown in the Duck Lake museum in Saskatchewan. Nowadays, even as in the 1800's, this tool would have to made by a blacksmith.

Gouge type of chisel which could be used for making round holes.

15

A broad axe is necessary if any hewing is to be done, such as in preparing the upper surfaces of joists and beams to receive flooring. As the name says, a broad axe is one with a very wide cutting edge. The face side is flat and it is sharpened from the other side only . . . something like a chisel. Nothing but a broad axe will make the straight-faced cut for a relatively even surface. Over the past several years, I have been intermittently working on a piece-en-piece building with all the members hewn on four sides for the framing. It is pleasant work which I do in easy stages on evenings and weekends. One day, while in a hurry, I used the chain saw and was surprised to find the finished member less exact than those logs which had been broadaxed. Furthermore, the surfaces were rough, whereas broadaxed surfaces are quite slick. (Building shown on previous page.)

These fine axes are difficult to obtain. So I am including, in a later section of this book on hewing, a dimensioned drawing so that a very good blacksmith may make one . . . although this is no easy task. When searching for a broadaxe to buy, remember that the weight of it means a great deal: it must not be less than 8 lbs., preferably 10 lbs. Anything lighter than this is more properly called a bench axe and is incapable of hewing logs. The broad axe should have about a 12" cutting edge and the older axes were forged of two metals, iron and steel. The iron formed the main bulk of the head, while the steel cutting edge was welded on. The advantage of this type of construction is that the axe can be more easily sharpened with the file and stone, and that, during the forging process, the axe can be more readily and precisely formed of the softer iron.

A chalk line is another necessary device for many jobs, including hewing. The type that reels back into a closed container filled with powdered, coloured chalk is good and can be obtained at any good hardware store.

An adze or lip adze can be a useful tool

but also a very dangerous one. Some expert builders use quite a varity of short handles adzes and axes. They can be handy but are not strictly necessary.

The builder will also need a peavey or

cant hook to move logs, 200 to 300 feet of ¾" polypropylene rope, and a single shive snatch block.

This list of tools is sufficient to construct a log building, but I would like to mention a chain saw attachment which enables an

individual to saw lumber. This is something to look into, not simply because of the high prices of lumber but also because of it frequently being such poor quality. There may be log-ends which could readily become excellent lumber. If you live in a region where popular and birch grow and are considered virtually weeds, you can make excellent finish lumber of them. Don't worry too much about making arbitrary commercial measurements such as 2x4 or 2x10 ... I find it a most welcome relief to see a good piece of wood that does not come off the usual assembly-line of shapes. It's best to consult with your local saw shop to see what they can provide for your particular make of saw.

How long does it take to build a log house?

A leisurely schedule might go this way, starting each spring as early as climatic conditions will allow. Year 1: site preparation, basement, drain-tile, septic tank installations and possibly the first round of logs with floor joists in place. After freeze-up or in mid-winter, fell the trees, skid them out cleanly on the snow, and transport them to the building site before load restrictions are imposed on the roads. Year 2: the logwork up to the point of having the roof on and fully weatherproof. Interior finishing may proceed all through the winter. Year 3: getting it all together, building the fireplace, pouring the driveways and sidewalks, installing the plumbing and electrical fixtures, the furnace, the floor coverings. And, before freeze-up, moving into a completely finished house.

This schedule might recommend itself to those who must build in their spare time. Certainly, the building of a log house need not take such a long time. I have built the logwork in a 30 x 40 ft. residence in a weekend, with the help of a very good man and a crew of students peeling the logs and sending them up to us. But somewhere in between these two extremes, there is a schedule to fit each project. Something to protect against is too high an expectation of how soon it will be finished. Work hard, but remember that it's a big project. As one builder told me, "I learned a lot of patience, building my first log house." I've seen people very discouraged, after a long summer of hard work, that they weren't moved in and toasting their knees in front of a fireplace. Yet they'd done extremely

well, and just didn't realize it. So it may be easier on the old ulcer to expect it might take three summers … and be pleasantly surprised if it does not.

One suggestion that can sometimes save half a year involves pre-building. If, for example, you purchase property in winter and can't possibly prepare the basement or foundation before many months go by, it is possible to begin the logwork with the idea of transporting it to

the basement and reassembling it, when all is ready. Sometimes this can be done in the woods where the trees are felled, and while it does cause a slight amount of extra work, i.e., putting the logs up twice, it eliminates a lot of work, too. All the bark, tops, and debris can be piled and burned

on the spot, and need never cause a moment's clutter around the homesite. But, if there is sufficient room on the property, it can also be done near the homesite. Before dismantling, mark each log end with a letter and a number indicating first, which corner it belongs to, and second, which number it is from the bottom. I use aluminum strips, imprinted with the symbols, and nailed to the log ends, to avoid any chance of the numbering being washed or rubbed off. It is also necessary to draw a sketch on which these symbols are recorded, as it could be a terrible thing to try and sort through a log pile, trying out one log after another, to find the one that fits in next.

The very shortest length of time, from blueprint to moving into a log home, is probably a year. That is even with a Contractor and plenty of help laid on. Solid timber construction isn't "instant housing" … it shouldn't be rushed.

How much does it cost to build a log house?

Again, the log house defies the production-line procedures of cost analysis. Everything depends on how much of the material the builder is able to obtain at little or no cost, such as the logs, the shakes, the rocks, the lumber … and how much of the labour the family is able to do themselves, also at little or no cost. Only the individual homeowner can get these figures and tot them up, and to help him, he might try to obtain regular estimating sheets that builders use, on which every conceivable item is listed. In general, it is only to be expected that the more one does or obtains for oneself, the less it costs … and at the other end of the scale, if everything is to be done by a Contractor the project can be expected to cost more than standard frame construction. Nor is this unreasonable since, in my opinion, the homeowner is getting a great deal more value.

Financing

The family hoping to live their lives at peace with nature should be free, independent, and in charge of their own destiny. To my mind, this means land and a home which is their own completely. For this reason, I am opposed to the borrowing of mortgage money. Because there is an abundance of advertising persuading people to borrow, I would like to mention here only a few points which surface usually when it's too late: the reasons why borrowing should be avoided. Most borrowers are convinced by the argument that a loan will give them freedom. My premise is that borrowing destroys freedom. It might be called volunteer slavery.

First, prime mortgage money is loaned only to those people willing to live on the reservation. This is understandable if a system, such as a city, is needed for "employment", to tax and regulate peoples' lives. The city works closely with the mortgage corporations. Federal money underwrites sewage systems which assure the optimum discharge into the rivers and lakes and oceans. Comical as it may seem (were it not so tragic) the federal housing money is then restricted entirely to those citizens willing to pollute the rivers, lakes, and oceans. And the cities work to maintain the sewers and to restrict and control housing hooked onto those pipes. In some way that continues to elude me, it assures an attractive profit on mortgage investments. It just won't

work on country homes, the official explained to me one day. So, in many respects, a good mortgage is like an Indian Treaty inasmuch as freedom is replaced by a lifestyle which an authorized official has decided would be better for people in general. No longer able to keep a horse or grow food, we take our treaty money to the Company stores. As the Indian people try to tell us, the full costs are not simply cash ... there is a high cost in pride, initiative, and the creativity which gives health to a family and to a nation. Once we become dependent, we are at the mercy of the supplier. So it seems to me that cities and mortgages are crippling people.

A family determined to live outside the city limits can certainly find a money lender to mortgage their land and future home, but the interest rate is higher. And in order to qualify, the rural family must also prove itself to be plugged into the economic system in such a way as to be receiving treaty money on a steady basis, to a level acceptable to the lender, and preferably month-by-month. The mortgage company is entirely justified in demanding such evidence for they, too, are plugged into that relentless system of cash-flow-or-out-you-go; they haven't time to understand about self-sufficiency or free-lancing or ecological survival: they need the dollars which fuel their computers and their financers. That's business. But the human family cannot be viewed strictly as a business. It has far deeper, more spiritual needs ... and a fine sense of achievement, rewarded by independence, is the goal which most of us are seeking. I'm suggesting only that it is possible to achieve that goal.

Another disadvantage of borrowing money is that the mortgage company will

very likely dictate a stereotyped interior floorplan. For example a house of less than 1,000 square feet, even if it is being built for a single person, has been taboo in many planning districts. Three bedrooms have been almost mandatory, as the president of a construction firm discovered when he applied for a conventional mortgage to cover a one-bedroom urban home for himself and his wife. His application was refused. "We wanted a very large living room and an extra large dining room, as we enjoy entertaining," he said, "but we simply didn't need more than one bedroom." So, knowing what he wanted, he went ahead and built the house with his own funds, in the way which pleased him and his wife. As conditions stand, anyone who cannot fit themselves into the restrictions of a business view of their lives, still has this option of going it alone ... before everything not forbidden has become mandatory.

The third disadvantage is the cost of a mortgage. A mortgage is an I.O.U. with a blackjack attached, explains freelance writer, Tom Alderman in THE CANADIAN magazine. Take for example, if you had obtained a $40,000.00 mortgage loan in 1976 at 12% with payments to be spread over 35 years. By the time you are through paying it off, sometime in 2011, you will have forked over a total of $166,733.83. Accept the fact, he says, that interest is loaded on at the front end of your mortgage. On a 35-year mortgage, the principal doesn't count for more than the interest until you've been paying for 29 years. Or, put it another way: after 10 years of payments totalling $47,649.60, you would have paid off just $1,521.65 of the actual debt. You haven't even bought the garage; all else was interest. You pay $3 in interest for every $1 you borrow.

If money is time, and time is what the days of our lives are made of, consider further that your debt must be paid from earnings ... and if you have a $20,000 a year job, you do not receive 20,000 real dollars -- or $1 for every $1 earned. After deductions, you are lucky if you receive 80¢ on the dollar. It's a tough climb up that mountain of debt.

The cost? Not just $166,733.83 ... but all the days when perhaps you should have been with your family or playing 'cello or sculpting or growing pumpkins or whatever is the sweet gift you have to give. That, in my opinion, is the intolerable cost of any financial indebtedness.

Before construction is considered, all possibilities should be explored for going it alone. Perhaps a year's leave of absence from paid employment would result in a debt-free house ... and enormous longterm savings. Or perhaps weekend and evening work might provide a small guest cottage in which the family could spend the first year. If only a small amount of money is available, I would again point out that my first house, on Francois Lake, cost $200 in cash to build. We did own the land and from it took our trees. The most beautiful of cedar shake roofing can be cut in many areas from free wood. Poplar and birch are similarly available and can provide fine flooring and finishing lumber. A few temporary discomforts, while a family lives in a guest cottage in order to get the big house going, is surely not as harmful as the constant anxiety and fear of being unable to meet heavy mortgage payments, and losing the home, if one's health or job fails. Temporary discomforts

of this nature deserve a better name ... involvement, perhaps. Or commitment. Or self-reliance. Independence. Pride!

Aim, above all, to buy the homesite outright in order to own completely whatever is built, grown, and created thereon. This truly is the key to freedom. It may also be the key to survival. That any Canadian should ever have to worry as to how he can acquire enough land for a home is a nightmare. Canadians can no longer readily afford or obtain what is, I believe, rightfully theirs alone: the soil of their homeland. But hopefully, hard determined shopping will find some land that can be paid for in full ... and hard determined legislation will, someday soon, protect for Canadians the land that they need. For only with land of your own can you truly hope to live in a log home the way it deserves to be lived in ... at peace with nature and as a legacy to the family's own future. A mortgage company might offer to do it all for you, yes ... but in my opinion, if they must cramp the size and shape of the house, restrict its location, narrow down its surroundings, dictate the family lifestyle with regard to its method of earning a living, and classify the quality of the neighbourhood in much the same manner, well, that is a price far too high to consider.

The site

Any home -- be it brick, plywood, stone, or whatever -- is situated most ideally on spacious, parklike grounds. Any home. Take any of the conventional modern houses out of a subdivision and set it down on wide lawns among shade trees (knock a few more windows into its two blank walls) and it would look twice the house it was in town. So if the Lawg Caybun concept is struggling fiercely,

trying to confine solid timber houses to certain regions and to restrict it from entering into others, it is well to consider how much better any home looks in the country, not just the log home. It was because I grew so heartily tired of the dogma that it shouldn't be done (''Can you get a building permit to put up a log house?'' people have asked me ... and ''Will they **let** you build a log house in a city?!'') that I decided that the College project for 1973-1974 had to be an urban house. So it is situated on an ordinary city

598 Kerry St., Prince George
1800 sq. ft. urban residence in round log construction. Douglas fir, cedar shake roof, local granite fireplaces. Maple leaf in leaded glass over entrance. CM&HC financed. B. Allan Mackie, 1974.

lot, surrounded by new houses in the upper-middle price range ... and I am more convinced than ever that, if I had to live right in town, I would prefer to do so in a log house. Most visitors to this project have agreed. In fact, voluntary offers to purchase the house were being deposited with the College bursar even before the basement was poured. It is possible in most towns in Western Canada to find log homes ... Jasper being one of the best examples I can think of ... and there are a great many fine timber-framed homes in the East, less easy to identify because they are usually sheathed. But it is self-limiting to suppose that a family that loves a log home is not going to be permitted to have one if they happen to like living in a city.

Choosing the site should, therefore, be done exactly as it is done for any fine home: for its personal appeal to the inhabitants, convenience, availability, and so on. Nobody would knowingly place a new home close to a highrise or a shopping plaza (would they?) and certainly not close to a high density traffic area, but if, 50 years from now, "progress" did suddenly expropriate an area, marking the houses for demolition -- none but the log house could be dismantled, moved, and reassembled in a new location, and be all the better for it!

The blueprint

Housing should be a very personal matter and I urge people always to make their proposed home as much a product of individual study and selection as possible. Sometimes additional help is needed ... and there is no substitute for expert advice. If a log building contractor is being hired, he or she may be the best person to draw the finished blueprints with a clear understanding of the engineering required for the special characteristics of logs. There is real peril in commissioning an architect or draftsman to do the job, if they have never studied log construction. It can double the labour costs, give longterm maintenance problems, and place great stress on the owner-builder relationship. As time goes on, there are more designer-draftsmen capable of giving you the help you need. I can handle only a limited number of custom jobs a year and I prefer the luxury of an unusual or challenging project. So in response to continued requests, I have completed a book, LOG HOUSE PLANS, in which 37 fully detailed designs are shown. Using this book, you may copy a plan directly from it; you may draw up your original designs guided by its instructions, or, for a nominal fee, you may order any of the 37 designs mailed to you. Remember that a simple alteration can also be drawn right onto these prepared blueprints if it better suits your needs ... as long as it is not a major structural change.

A square building, for example, is probably the easiest to build and can be the most efficient in the amount of space enclosed for the least available materials. It may also have less exposed area relative to the usable floor area. A variety of wall lengths will make better use of the available material, however, so it is more likely that even a modest plan will be made into a rectangle not only for the appearance but also for better interior arrangements. The problem for the novice to understand, so that he keeps the two long and two short walls level as he builds, is that it can be done by using logs of an average mean diameter. That is, the midpoint diameter of the short logs

should be the same as the midpoint diameter of the long ones. This, of course holds true for partition walls of log, too.

Any design calling for a very long, straight wall is almost certain to cause difficulty in the horizontal log method. Some form of bracing or support should be incorporated every 16 to 20 feet of horizontal log wall. This can be done by creating a jog partway along the wall, thus permitting two logs to be used where the single long one might have been. Another answer is to incorporate stub walls halfway along, preferably at either side of a door or window. Partitions also perform this cross-bracing function. Or, another way to put in a long, straight, but safe log wall is to employ the French-Canadian method of piece-en-piece construction.

Floor-to-ceiling windows are something to ponder well, before including in a log house plan. I never feel right about cutting out an entire wall from top to bottom. I like to see the visible interlock of the logs. Only skilled carpentry and careful attention to structural support can make such large windows possible. So reconsider, beforehand, whether the window really should be that large. Corner windows, for these same structural reasons, should not be planned. A great deal of the stubborn strength of a log house is in its interlocking corners. I have always liked that story about the Peace River grandma. After the family had become well-to-do and built a fine modern stucco farmhouse, she grew ever more ashamed and resentful of the old log home standing out behind. It had sheltered them through all the hardships, the children had grown up in that house, and as grown men they refused to let it be disturbed. So one day, when the menfolk were in town on business, this foxy grandma got a bulldozer operator over. She meant to have that old log house demolished and burned before sundown. It was one of her sons who told me the story. "We got home late that night," he said, shaking his head, "and there was this guy on a cat, with his headlights on, chasing that old log house all over the farm. He'd been at it all day. It just wouldn't fall down!" So it is better, I think, to take advantage of strength like that. And while it could be possible to make substitutes which would permit part of the massive corners to be replaced by glass, I wouldn't.

Perhaps the most important difference in log house design and planning lies in the fact that logs settle. They will shrink approximately ½" to each log, and the whole wall will settle down, bedding ever more firmly together, for at least 2 years and often longer. A tall wall, being heavier, is going to settle down a little more, in total, than does a wall of moderate height. Therefore, the essential precaution is to provide enough open header space above all the doors, windows, and partitions, anywhere that the logs could come down on and get hung up. Be most particularly watchful with upright posts of any kind. It was with good reason that the old French and British builders clung to their belief in the superior strength of the upright log. The enormous weight of a log building coming down on an interior post can drive it right through the floor unless sufficient free space is left so that this can't happen. It is wise to check up on how much settling is taking place, during those first few years, as it is not at all difficult to make a few judicious cuts, and perhaps remove a bit more wood with a slick or a chisel, in order to release the pressure. Otherwise logs can be forced out of position or the hangup will lift logs enough to open up spaces along a wall.

The electrical wiring layout must be detailed completely in the blueprint because the wires have to be installed very early in the logwork. Heating and plumbing systems, too, should be fully laid out in the blueprint so as to make sure that ducts or pipes do not conflict with beams in any way. Pre-planning is the only sure way to end up with these ugly intestinal lines being concealed properly. They are not ornamental.

With these few factors in mind, however, it should be possible to adapt almost any good houseplan to logs. The standard ones which might be unsatisfactory are those with very small rooms and those with too many partitions. Eliminating some of the partitions might solve both problems but, in any event, let the rooms of a log house be spacious. Similarly, the height of the ceilings should be expanded. Not only is there the settling factor to consider, which means that the ceiling will -- within the first two years -- be at least 5" lower than it appears when new. But there is also the massiveness of the log ceiling beams, which makes them appear overpowering if they are not lifted to about 8 ft. (measuring from the underside of the beams). Err on the side of making it too high, rather than discovering, too late, that it's too low. There's great temptation to "Let it go at that," as you come up to the 9th or 10th round of logs. But, if in doubt, put on another round. You'll be thankful ever after, that you did.

Exterior design is more difficult, but also rewarding. About all one can say is to strive to blend the house into the landscape. This is not to say, strive to make the house look like all other houses as so many professional "planners" consciously aim to do, in cities. Rather, try to be in harmony with the natural colouring and contours of the landscape. A house which succeeds in this is especially beautiful and, of course, the log house always has a head start when it comes to blending with nature. Reading the architectural philosophy of Arthur Erickson will help greatly.

Planning a good home

Consider, at all times, who you are building for. I deplore the building of a house for its so-called resale value, a terrible contradiction in the meaning of a home, but a big stick which mortgage companies and real estate firms hold over the heads of the public. It seems to me, however, that if a house is planned to give maximum joy and comfort to a certain family, another family will be eager to buy it. So plan for real feelings and human needs. Discarding those strategems intended to line us all up in rows, looking and behaving all alike, your task is to see the function and purpose of a good home. Analyse how you live and how you'd like to live. Sketch, discuss, measure, read, investigate. It is not impossible that you might discover your personal concept of pleasing space is one very large room. If so, take courage. Erickson lives in just such a house with a blank wall turned to one of Vancouver's most fashionable streets.

The Silloep Hill Ranch House

The Silloep Hill house shown in the houseplan below is given, here, as an example of planning to meet very unusual circumstances. If I explain how the design developed, and why, it may help others in analyzing and designing for their special, and different, needs. There was no blueprint on the market for a house which could function smoothly for six months at a stretch without a trip to a grocery store. Unless extremely fortunate, your lifestyle may not require this kind of accommoda-

tion, but whatever the particular needs, the methods of enquiry, testing, and planning will be similar. Uppermost in our minds was the idea that our ranch house should serve its occupants rather than the occupants serving the house through constant repairs, painting, polishing, or by submitting our free movement to any avoidable obstacle or inconvenience.

The Silloep Hill Ranch, which my wife and I homesteaded in 1959, required a house adapted to the climate, the isolation, and the scenery of this area of north-central British Columbia. Like most people intending to build, we first looked

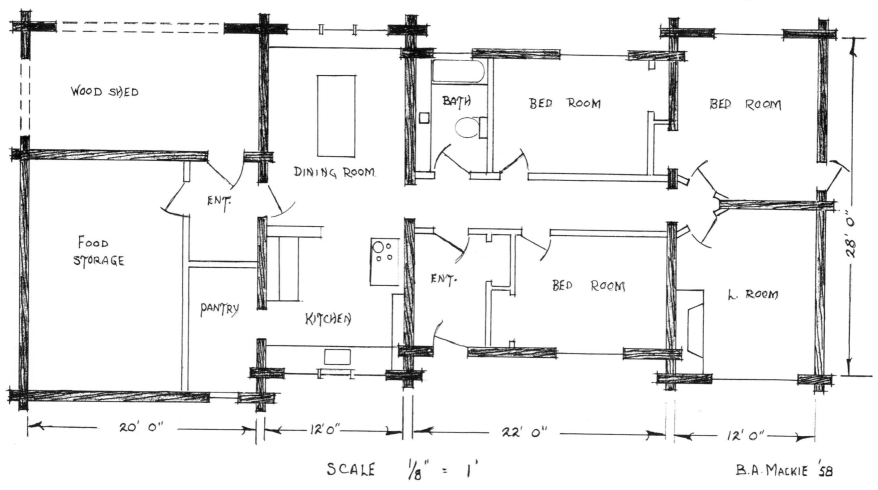

WOOD SHED

DINING ROOM.

ENT.

FOOD STORAGE

PANTRY

KITCHEN

BATH

BED ROOM

BED ROOM

ENT.

BED ROOM

L. ROOM

28' 0"

20' 0"   12' 0"   22' 0"   12' 0"

SCALE 1/8" = 1'

B.A. MACKIE '58

at books of houseplans. But even after special enquiries to C.M. & H.C., public libraries, and UBC, we found no plans for a true working ranch house. All plans were variations of the city bungalow with larger houses simply running to luxury rooms for formal entertainment or recreation rather than to work space or food storage. We knew that no compact kitchen could shelve all our provisions any more than dinette space could accommodate a branding crew. Nor did we anticipate any formal entertaining, our visitors arriving unannounced by ones, twos, or a family group. The university librarians worked diligently but were able to send us only generalized information as to how to judge the efficiency of a kitchen (quite helpful) plus their good wishes. As homesteaders, my wife and I had no

choice but to research and develop our own houseplan. Once having done so, I recommend it to anyone hoping for a home to be more than the standard cubicles in which we eat, sleep, and watch television.

The key to all the unusual features of the Silloep Hill houseplan was its isolation. We undertook the homesteading of new country in the belief that solitude is a privilege. But we felt that the adequate provisioning and smooth functioning of the household were essential to the fullest appreciation of this idyllic life. Thus, the Silloep Hill house is large, to ensure that it served generously its functions as home, school and office -- virtually everything -- to a family of four. All supplies including firewood were stored under the ranch house roof. This

convenience, plus a complete absence of steps would, we hoped, prevent our having to depart for "easier" living in our old age.

Isolation dictated massive food storage areas. Isolation also made more subtle demands such as providing room for the whole family to work comfortably together indoors. It also indicated that, if we were to avoid irritations now and then, there should be a room where each member of the family could pursue work or study completely uninterrupted. And so that isolation need not mean boredom, we arranged for all possible viewing of the horizon and Nadina Mountain. These were the basic modifications.

Climate, we thought, indicated that entry halls should be incorporated into both the front and back door entries so as

to afford double-door protection from cold. The back entrance was further incorporated into the woodshed, permitting severely mudded boots to be kicked off, coats to be doffed, or snow brushed off quite comfortably before even a door was opened. The kitchen was central, its long walls protected. We called this room our fortress and I built two bunks as window seats into the dining end of the kitchen so that no blizzard or furnace failure could catch us without an answer. The climate turned out to be milder than expected but these plans made the house all the more comfortable.

In the final plan, some conventional rooms had shrunk while others expanded enormously. For example, our living room dwindled to a retreat measuring 12x14, suitable for private conversation or reading. As its purpose was restfulness, it faced away from the exciting sweep of mountain scenery and looked, instead, onto trees and quiet pastures. This usually had to be explained to guests who, if they were city people, asked three standard questions: why didn't you build your house right on the public road instead of two miles in? why is your house so big? and why doesn't your living room face the view? Peace, peace, peace ... that's why.

Our kitchen was naturally the room which expanded. The main room was 12x28 with three adjoining units: a pantry for all dry food storage, a double-walled rootcellar for all the vegetables and canned goods, plus a woodshed. In the kitchen itself, my wife could be cooking, the children could play, and I could be mending a saddle all at the same time and comfortably. Visitors to any ranch head straight for the kitchen. Usually having travelled far they are cold, hungry, weary.

In this big room they could warm their hands over the kitchen stove or relax at the dining table while coffee or a meal was being prepared. It's an unhappy cook who, living in isolation, is denied these welcome social contacts because of a "compact" kitchen.

How did we know the size of rooms needed? Our method of developing the room sizes involved 1) observing certain old ranch houses, some of which were extremely comfortable and efficient; 2) from imagining ourselves into the blueprint and visualizing entire sequences of indoor activity; 3) from using bits of cardboard, drawn to scale, to represent our tables, chairs, beds, shuffling these on the houseplan to get a surprisingly clear idea of how work and play would feel in the spaces we had arranged.

Personal planning pays many rewards. Efficiency is one. Not content with having storage for food and fuel, we saw ways to make the longterm handling of these items much easier. Simply by enlarging all doors, I could run a wheelbarrow of vegetables right from the garden indoors to the storage bins in the rootcellar. Twice a day, a wheeled woodbox also went gliding through this door to take on a load of wood without our every having to carry any in our arms. Another great help was a bake counter tailored to hold all the cooking equipment and materials within arm's reach, with an appropriate counter height eliminating the strain of kneading bread dough or stirring cake batter. (The small children also made good use of this low counter.) In this bake centre, at my wife's request, I installed no cupboard doors as I had once counted the number of times she opened and closed them (14!) in the preparation of a simple afternoon tea. In fact, any door or

partition must nowadays account for itself in solid terms before it is allowed into our home. If it serves no purpose such as warmth or privacy, these clearly are not doors or partitions -- they are merely obstacles.

By the time we moved into the Silloep Hill ranch house, we had thought it all out so carefully we knew exactly where every item belonged and how to get right to work. It was a good home, but when I say that planning is a very personal thing, a matter of individual need and feeling, I can perhaps best explain this by saying that I would not build that house exactly the same way today, as I did in 1959. Conditions have changed. It is no longer so isolated in the Owen Lake region. We have changed. We are cured of wanting a large herd of beautiful cattle only to see them shipped to slaughter. And furthermore, society has changed. In 1959 there was much in the public attitude that made us willing to forego a great deal that society offered. But today, although formal entertaining may never be a feature of our wilderness, we do find so much that is hopeful in the general outlook especially among young people that we would expect to incorporate much of the "outside" world -- visitors, guests, students, workers -- into a good home there now.

The Southbank House at Francois Lake

This house might be used to illustrate that a house need be neither expensive nor complicated in order to be a good home. It is essentially a single large room, the function and purpose of which was to permit all possible viewing of the beautiful lake at the doorstep. Minimum partitions separated the two sleeping areas so that the big windows facing north could be seen from anywhere in the house at all times. This meant that by merely lifting our heads off the pillow at night we might be rewarded by seeing the northern lights sweeping the sky or the dawn's pink light flooding the ice. I never saw a door or a partition to equal such sights.

The Southbank house might be considered more romantic than practical unless viewed in terms of cash alone. It cost us little more than the price of a month's rent in an average city apartment. Or, for that matter, scarcely more than a month's mortgage payment.

Finally, to assist the person trying for the first time to express his own needs in housing, I would offer reassurance derived from Arthur Erickson: that there is really no such thing as ''good design'' or ''pleasing design'' ... a good, pleasing building is concerned with meaning, and ''the strength and simplicity of a building is achieved through clarity of meaning.''

THE HOUSE ON FRANCOIS LAKE

Acquisition of logs

There are three ways to obtain a sufficient number of straight logs of uniform and suitable size: from your own property, from Crown land, or from a commercial log producer. Ideally you will have the trees on your own property, although great care should be taken that the woods surrounding your new home will not be depleted.

To cut trees from Crown lands, a Free Use permit is applied for through the nearest B. C. Forest Service office. Under Section 25 of the Forest Act, this permit is readily issued without charge to a Canadian citizen who is a settler engaged in agriculture, or who holds a Free Miner's licence, and who does not have sufficient timber on his own land for the purpose specified in the permit. This Free Use permit is a privilege maintained from the past and should be jealously guarded. A Special Use permit may also be obtained and the payment of a reasonable stumpage and royalty is required for the trees cut. Often a forest district will have a Special Sale area set up, on which it is possible to harvest fence posts, cedar shake blocks, firewood, or whatever material the area offers. Suitable house logs may sometimes be obtained here. But as Crown lands come more and more under the control of large corporations, the individual is forced to get his logs from a commercial producer. If you are obliged to do this, you will undoubtedly find several logging companies listed in the telephone directory. After talking to a few of them, you'll be able to tell which operator can or will supply properly selected logs delivered to the building site. Large logging companies may not be interested in sorting out ideal trees. Smaller outfits are usually more obliging this way.

To buy logs, you need only specifiy the lengths, sizes, and species, as well as the number required. Purchased logs will be scaled and charged for by the cunit (100 cubic feet). A log 28 feet long, 9'' at the top and 12'' at the butt will contain 17 cubic feet or about 5 logs per cunit. Prices will vary among the individual logging operators depending upon weather conditions and how busy they are. Prices can also vary with the same operator, from time to time, according to the kind of area he happens to be logging in. You can expect to pay more if it is at all difficult for them to sort out the required

number of good house logs. When placing your order, be generous in your estimates of the log lengths. Allow at least 5 or 6 feet beyond the actual wall length to provide ample material for finishing the log ends and also to overcome the danger of a too-short log coming off the walls when it is being rolled across the building, and one end of it falling into the interior.

Selection of logs

If the building is to be about 30 feet square, suitable logs might be 14 to 16 inches at the butt. So if you are selecting the trees yourself, mark those which measure between 42 and 48 inches in girth. As a general rule, small buildings require smaller logs; large buildings seem to demand larger ones. If in doubt, always err on the side of bigness for not only do the logs shrink but the added size is helpful in several ways -- thicker and therefore better insulated walls, fewer notches to cut, a more solid appearance and, of course, superior strength.

To judge if a tree is straight, first look at it from a distance of about 100 feet and from two sides, at right angles to each other. If no sweep or crook can be seen in the required length, move in close and sight up the tree. It must be very straight to appear so from this angle. Few trees are perfectly straight and, in my opinion as a builder, this is good. I admire an axeman courageous enough to use big, rugged trees. Such logs have great beauty, similar to that achieved in a roof of rough, hand split shakes. This should be considered in comparison to some machine peeled logs which become so perfectly alike as to seem like a package of drinking straws. The use of massive and imperfectly shaped logs requires maximum skill on the part of the builder. Such a house should be highly valued not only for its strength of character and dramatic naturalness, but also for the craftsmanship which it requires. The beginner, however, is well advised to use the straightest trees available.

Species

Almost any species of tree that grows to log size can be made into a building. But some, because of their characteristic form, durability, or colour are more desirable than others. In British Columbia, in loose order of preference, the most suitable trees for logs, floor joists, rafters, and shakes are cedar or Douglas fir, pine, spruce, hemlock, and balsam. After seeing hewn poplar buildings in Saskatchewan still standing true and square after almost a century, I would hesitate to say that even these trees, so unappreciated here, are not worthy of consideration. But the **Western Red Cedar** is very durable and young trees have very good form for log building. These will be difficult to find in most areas and very expensive to buy since they are always in great demand as power poles. **Douglas fir** is very strong and durable wood. The trees often have a distinct sweep. They make excellent rafters, joists, ridgepoles, as well as logs. **Lodgepole Pine** have excellent form

and durability and are easy to cut and peel. **Engelman Spruce** is a white soft wood and not as durable as the others when exposed to weathering conditions. Kept dry, it is quite serviceable, generally is very straight, and is easy to work with. **Western Hemlock** has good form and is sufficiently durable if kept dry. It is difficult to find completely sound wood, however, since it is very susceptible to decay. **Balsam** is also a very soft wood and is subject to decay if not well protected. While suitable for building, it is not preferred.

How to fall a tree

An early immigrant to this country was asked which way the tree he was chopping was expected to fall. "How should I know," he replied indignantly, "I'm not a bloody prophet!" He must have been surprised when he learned he could indeed have influenced the outcome. The term "faller", rather than wood-cutter or some such name, does indicate where the skill is centred. Cutting through a tree seems simple enough. But to lay that tree safely on the ground, unspoiled and precisely where it is wanted, is the skill of one who cuts down trees.

The faller, first of all, determines the direction of the lean or weight of the tree in respect to the stump. Hopefully, it leans the same direction you want it to fall ... and you want it to fall where it can be tied onto at the top for skidding out. So if it leans not too heavily in some other direction, it may be wedged into the correct lean by driving a magnesium or plastic faller's wedge into the back cut at the right time and place. But if the tree is leaning too heavily in the wrong direction,

you would be wise to fall it that way even though it will be harder to skid.

Next, check your "getaway" path ... a clear trail to a safe place (nearly always to one side and behind the stump in respect to the direction of fall) where you're out of the way of the tree butt or any debris which may be thrown back.

To begin cutting, place the undercut on the side toward which you expect the tree to fall. The depth of the undercut should be ¼ to ⅓ of the diameter of the tree. In height, the undercut should be ⅓ the depth. Make this cut as close to the ground as possible. The backcut is put in next, parallel to the undercut and 1" to 2" higher on the tree. As soon as the saw blade is fully into the tree, a wedge may be placed in the cut to hold it open in case there has been any slight miscalculation as to which way the tree was leaning. Continue the back cut to within 1" of the undercut on moderately sized trees. This inch is called the "hinge wood".

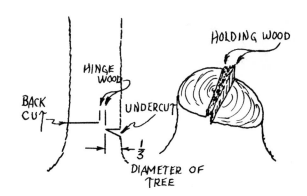

The tree should begin to fall in the direction of the undercut. If it does not, check that the cuts are straight and true, then drive the wedge with the back of the axe more firmly into place, thus lifting the tree into the desired direction. On a stubborn tree, use two wedges. If the tree is leaning to one side of the chosen direction where the undercut has been placed, it is a good idea to leave a little extra thickness of hinge wood on the offside. This holding wood tends to direct the tree more accurately into the right path. Once the tree begins its fall, take the saw and make immediate use of your getaway path. If the saw sticks in the cut, leave it! Do not waste precious seconds tugging at it, when the saw will likely come to no harm and is replaceable, anyway. Watch the tree to the ground for, as it falls, it may brush other tree tops, bending them for a distance. As these tops swing back into position, they may throw limbs or chunks in your direction. These limbs are called "widowmakers" for good reason. Also, as the tree hits the ground the butt may recoil into the air, or other wood that it hits may fly up. Watch and anticipate these possibilities so that you may step clear. And if the tree comes to rest woven between others, be very cautious how you treat it. A heavily bound tree can possess tremendous power. Be in the clear when you make a release cut or, if it appears too dangerous, get an experienced friend to help. Finally, wear a hard hat. Never leave partly cut trees standing. Do not fall trees on a windy day. And never go out alone to fall timber. But otherwise, you could say there's nothing to it; it's easy as falling off a log.

When to cut. Peeling of logs.

Logs are best cut in winter when the sap is down in the tree. Logs may be skidded readily and cleanly on the snow, with much less danger of mechanical damage. If winter cutting is impossible, the next best times are late fall and, after that, summer. But spring cutting is the least preferable ... even though spring-cut logs do peel much more readily. The disadvantage is that they are so heavy with sugary sap in this season, they are very susceptible to mildew and staining. Being swollen, they seem more susceptible to subsequent checking, too. The Scandinavian log builders of old had many techniques for seasoning logs without checking. The most amazing I have read about was their method of topping the standing trees, leaving two limbs, then peeling two strips of bark down the sides as the workman returned to the ground; the tree was felled after it stood, like this, for about two years. Such precaution accounts for the beautiful condition of some of their buildings dating from the 1300s. In my own woods experience, I have noted that a tree which might have been bulldozed off a new road, for example, and has been down for a year but with its roots and limbs still intact, does appear to have seasoned much better than a tree cut and limbed and stored for a year. I am not at all sure why we, in this era of mechanical aids and conveniences, have so much less time to spare for these refinements than did workmen of 600 years ago. It is something I often ponder. We rush about at top speed, working, with all kinds of gadgetry to help us, and we accomplish less. But if you are interested in optimum sesoning of logs, it would appear to occur in much the same manner as a tree's natural death would occur and must, therefore, take at least two years. I strongly urge against felling the building logs and immediately peeling them. Don't peel a log until you are ready to set it on the building. Even if the logs, for unforeseen reasons, must be stored one or even two years, don't peel them. The bark is the best protection I have seen against mildew, checking, weathering, and mechanical damage. Logs stored for two years with the bark on will, yes, acquire bark beetles and a certain amount of staining. I have many such ones in my own home and we like their patterns.

Storage of logs

Many people ask how long the logs should be stored, before they are used. I have come to the conclusion that to stack logs for seasoning is to overlook their ability to take a "set" as they dry. In fact, it creates a problem, as they will take a set according to the logpile in which they were stored. Far better that they should be put into the building as green logs so that, as they dry and set, they take on the alignment that the builder is working so hard to achieve. I have often cut a tree down and put it on a building the same day. Ideally, the logwork should be allowed to dry and season, thereafter, for a year -- that is, as walls without windows and doors to impede the free movement of air and to keep the temperature the same both indoors and out. But while it would be ideal to have the building wait a year to dry and season, it is not entirely necessary ... usually, by the time the roof is finished, it has had time for the largest part of the drying to take place. Remember, of course, that green logs would require plenty of header space above all doors, windows, and partitions, to avoid settling hangups.

If it is not possible to store the logs in the form of the walls, perhaps because the foundation work cannot be completed until spring, then they should be decked (without peeling) in tiers. Use two or more skids, depending on the lengths. Skids are simply small logs laid on the ground or between layers. If logs are piled more than one tier high, the skids should be positioned directly over the ones below so that the weight of the upper logs will not bend the lower ones.

Checking problems are reduced to almost zero if the bark is left on the log until the moment it is ready to go up on the building. The direct hot sunlight, in some regions, can cause added checking and in this case, paint the logs down with a brine made by adding as much salt as can be dissolved in water. Applying linseed oil to the logs also curbs checking but since the oiling renders the log slippery underfoot, it can only be done when it won't create a hazard to those working on the building.

Safety

Much has been written about safety in general terms and I agree with most of it ... in particular, the point that safety is the responsibility of each individual. I choose this one because I know from experience that the farther you are removed from any hope of assistance, the fewer accidents occur. I think this is because you place the concern more squarely on your own shoulders, anticipating more fully the consequences of your movements. My wife and I spent six years with two small children in the Owen Lake area. We were 78 miles from the nearest doctor and 26 miles from a telephone, yet only twice came close to serious injury. The reason for this low incidence was, I believe, the added care used when it is not possible to

call for help. Thus, accidents can be avoided -- particularly if you understand the hazards. And there are a few hazards peculiar to working with logs. Here are some guidelines:

- Roll a log always toward the center of the building to work on it. A log near the edge could fall and take you with it.

- Stand outside the skids to adjust the angle of the log being raised. This way, if the rope comes loose or the skid slips, you are on the outside and clear to move to safety.

- "Don't stand in the bight!" This old logger's axiom means never to stand within the bend of a line under tension. Any failure in equipment when you are in this position places you in grave danger.

- Place sharp-edged tools well out of your way. If you plan to keep a tool such as the peavey or auger up on the top log, make sure it is driven firmly into a position where it cannot fall. Allow nobody to work or watch from below you. When your axe is not in use, drive it into the wall one log down with the blade flush to the wall so you cannot possibly bump into it or step on it.

- Before starting to chop, always take a slow practice swing with your axe to ensure that there is no obstruction to the backswing and that a glancing blow will endanger no one.

- Wear shoes that afford a good grip on the logs. Hard-toed caulk boots would be the ones recommended by my father who, in the days of the Barr Colonists of which he was one, drove a broad-axe between his great toe and second toe, cutting his boot and two pairs of sox but

not his skin. He took the rest of the day off, anyway.

Preparing the building site

The location of the building should be clearly in mind before any land clearing is done. This will not only protect the natural landscaping and shrubbery but will also be part of the plot plan drawing which the Building Inspector will probably require. With the clear idea of where the house will sit, it might be possible to prepare by hand the small area within the foundation line. Most back hoe operations disturb little of the surrounding trees. Some cat. operators can dig the basement with surprisingly little damage, too, if properly instructed and duly rewarded. Avoid laying waste to an acre of land, at any rate. It is worth a bundle, afterwards, in landscaping. Even within the ever-narrowing confines of a city lot, try to save any tree still brave enough to grow there by wrapping the trunks in burlap or by wiring a line of boards around them. If a tree does receive a scar, paint the wound to stop the "bleeding" of its vital fluids.

Generally, one corner or one wall is chosen as a starting point for the building's position. Erect batter boards around three corners and at least 4 feet beyond the outside of the foundation line. The corner can be squared by using a triangle measuring in the proportion of 3 and 4 on the sides and 5 on the hypotenuse. That is, the front line may be marked 20 feet (4x5 feet) beyond the chosen corner, the side line marked at 15 feet (3x5 feet) beyond where it crosses the corner location and adjusted until the hypotenuse measurement between them measures 25 feet (5x5 feet). The fourth batter boards may now be located by measurement and the squareness of the building checked by confirming that the diagonal measurements are within ¼″ of being equal. Other foundation lines may now be located easily by measurement.

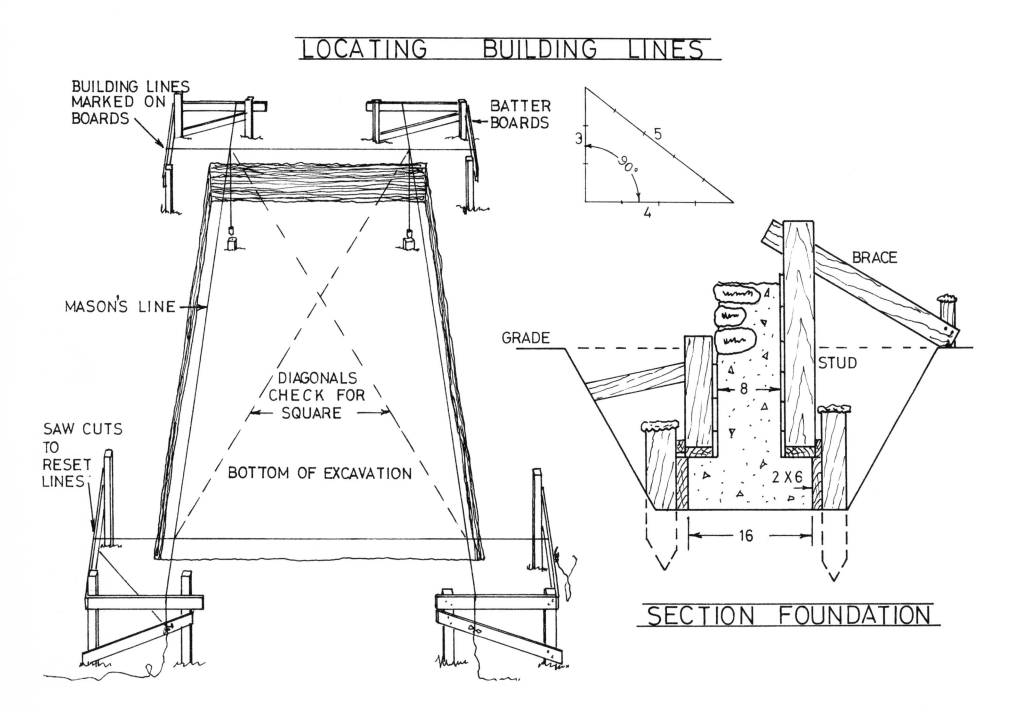

LOCATING BUILDING LINES

BUILDING LINES MARKED ON BOARDS

BATTER BOARDS

MASON'S LINE

DIAGONALS CHECK FOR SQUARE

SAW CUTS TO RESET LINES

BOTTOM OF EXCAVATION

3

5

90°

4

BRACE

GRADE

STUD

8

2 X 6

16

SECTION FOUNDATION

Foundations and basements

When an old log building falls into disrepair, it is largely because it was built without a proper foundation. This is an example of a building practice which the pioneer, under duress, was forced to do because of the limited materials available to him. His errors should never be our guideline, except to note the simple means we have today of avoiding such errors. His home probably had its first logs laid right on the ground or on small rocks (which he could carry) and which the weight of the building would soon drive into the earth, so that it had no hope of surviving long. Or his house may indeed have been set up on a large boulder or cedar pilings at the corners but then, for lack of insulating materials for the floors, the pioneer would be forced to bank up all around the foundations with earth which did assure a few draught-free winters but guaranteed the quick deterioration of the logs as well. Nowadays, it is quite simple to assure the maximum lifespan for any home by providing proper foundations and well-insulated floors . . . to start with. Indeed there's more involved, but the proper foundation is the essential beginning.

I must admit that I often find it difficult to follow, myself, the good advice which I'm now going to set forth. That it is excellent advice is undeniable. But there are many times when circumstances such as weather make it irresistibly tempting to try to by-pass the fundamentals of good preparation. Indeed, I have put in septic tanks and drain tile long after the building is completed. I've even helped people dig basements after the house if built. Each time I've wondered how anybody could be so lacking in foresight . . . but I see the same urge in others as well as myself: Let's get at it; let's get the roof on; let's worry about the details after that. Well, believe me, it's absolutely never easier to do any job later, never. And certainly it's never more efficient.

A foundation, to be good, need not be expensive or complicated . . . and I agree with Frank Lloyd Wright who considered basements to be expensive storage, poor root cellars, ugly, and unless they have good stairs and ample head room, a hazard to life and limb. In bygone days when hot air gravity furnaces were used -- and perhaps because of poorly drained sites -- it was felt that footings had to be dug down fairly deep and that only a little extra depth would supply much added space in the form of a full basement. Thus, almost by default, basements came to be considered an essential part of housebuilding. But frost affects foundation walls only if they are poorly drained. The need for footings has been greatly exaggerated. On a well drained or sloping site, drain rock compacted around drain tile is sufficient footing and concrete or masonry walls may be built directly upon this. However, this is a question which each builder appears to have to argue out with his local Building Inspector. Refer to the national building code (kept in all libraries, I believe) for guidance and support for what you'd like to build. A full concrete basement is becoming as extremely expensive "extra" if a family actually would prefer to live without one.

Low rockwork foundations are most complementary to log buildings. The inexperienced mason need not fear laying a rock faced wall if he places the inside half of the foundation form up first and

fits stone on the outside only, filling in between the stones and the foundation form with concrete as the wall goes up. In the foundation of the Silloep Hill ranch house, shown above, I used local rock, striving for an appearance of rough, artless solidness so that the finished foundation would be scarcely noticed.

A flat foundation is suggested for dry locations, to keep the building close to the ground. This may have a slab foor as illustrated on the following page, Fig. 5, or a footing as in Figs. 1, 2, or 3. A generous overhang will keep moisture away form the sloped wall. End walls may have 4 or 5" extra height added to them to meet the bottom of the end logs which will be higher than the side logs.

A prepared mixture called masonry cement is available to use with sand and water to make a mortar suitable for stonework. However, if the wall is to be filled behind the rock with concrete, it is just as well to use concrete between the rocks. Readymix cement will not be possible for the small amounts you will work with at any one time. But if you are

FOUNDATIONS

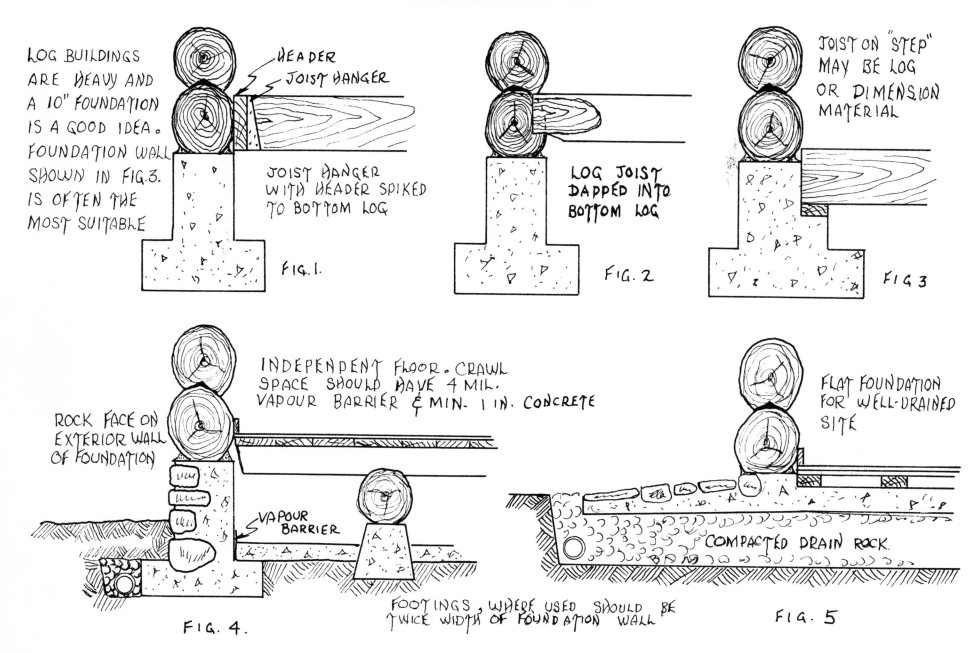

LOG BUILDINGS ARE HEAVY AND A 10" FOUNDATION IS A GOOD IDEA. FOUNDATION WALL SHOWN IN FIG. 3. IS OFTEN THE MOST SUITABLE

HEADER
JOIST HANGER

JOIST HANGER WITH HEADER SPIKED TO BOTTOM LOG

FIG. 1.

LOG JOIST DAPPED INTO BOTTOM LOG

FIG. 2

JOIST ON "STEP" MAY BE LOG OR DIMENSION MATERIAL

FIG 3

ROCK FACE ON EXTERIOR WALL OF FOUNDATION

INDEPENDENT FLOOR. CRAWL SPACE SHOULD HAVE 4 MIL. VAPOUR BARRIER & MIN. 1 IN. CONCRETE

VAPOUR BARRIER

FOOTINGS, WHERE USED SHOULD BE TWICE WIDTH OF FOUNDATION WALL

FIG. 4.

FLAT FOUNDATION FOR WELL-DRAINED SITE

COMPACTED DRAIN ROCK.

FIG. 5

33

in doubt about the quality of the material otherwise available, get your sand and gravel from a supplier. Both sand and gravel must be clean. This is easily checked by half filling a glass jar with the sand or gravel to be used. Let it stand overnight after adding water and shaking thoroughly. The material will have settled in strata with the light organic material on top. If the top layer of mud or organic material is more than 1/8'' thick the sand or gravel must be washed.

If it is not practical to obtain the use of a portable cement mixer, the job of mixing the cement can be done with a sweatboard. This is a platform about 6 ft. square. A few shovels of coarse and fine aggregate are placed in the centre of the platform and cement added. A ratio of 5 to 1 is generally adequate unless the aggregate is very fine. Mix the dry material first, then add the least possible amount of clean water to obtain a workable mix. This is hard work and mixes should be small if used for rockwork as this material sets up quickly.

First logs and floor joists

Concrete is considered to have

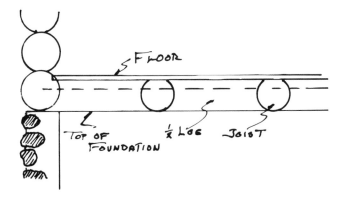

obtained full strength in 28 days, but it is not necessary to wait more than 5 days before carefully placing the first logs. The first logs will probably be ½ logs and may be either on the side walls or on the end walls. Some thought should be given to this. The choice will depend upon the kind of floor joists to be used -- whether log or 2 x 10 -- and just how the floor joists are carried on the foundation. In the example sketched at left, the log floor joists are resting on the foundation wall and at right angles to the first ½ logs. This permits the ends of the floor decking to rest comfortably on the sill log above the diameter line. When the floor joists are recessed into the masonry, other considerations such as span and beam location may become more important.

The butts should all face one way and the underside of each log is well flattened. Some builders have tried to put a 1'' layer of concrete on top of the foundation and sink the log into it. This is very hard to do. It is perhaps better to grout concrete around the log after the building has gained a few rounds in height.

The next logs should now be placed at right angles to these first ones, with the butts again all one way. If the foundation is not built up at the ends, this space can be grouted in when the side logs are done.

Now begins the job of notching the corners of the logs soundly together. When the first round is in place, you can cut out the notches for the floor joists if they are to be of logs also. In this case, a chalk line is run level the length of the side logs so as to locate the bottom bearing for the joists. Individual notches may be cut at 2-foot centres as shown at right, or a

full ''step'' may be cut with a chain saw to give a bearing surface about 2 or 3'' wide.

Log floor joists will be fair-sized logs of about 10 or 12'' diameter. After they have been hewn to obtain a flat surface of at least 2'' in width for the rough flooring, the joists may be cut to exact length. Next, flatten the under-surface for a few inches back from the end to make the joist height equal for all joists. By placing the joists at opposite ends of the run first, all the rest can be aligned to a chalk-line stretched between them.

If the span of the floor joists is greater than 10 ft., the floor may spring slightly. Bridging could be put in but is difficult. It's best to run another log down the center for them to rest on, and which can be supported in several places. Any unevenness of the bottoms can be taken care of with wedges.

Floor insulation is a necessity if a crawl space is not heated. Two possible solutions are illustrated on the next page, although many other alternatives could be used to obtain the optimum R-value and to ensure that a vapour barrier exists, between the house and the insulation.

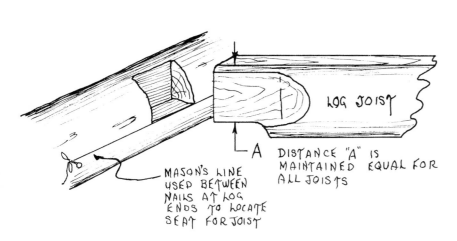

LOG JOIST

A

MASON'S LINE USED BETWEEN NAILS AT LOG ENDS TO LOCATE SEAT FOR JOIST

DISTANCE "A" IS MAINTAINED EQUAL FOR ALL JOISTS

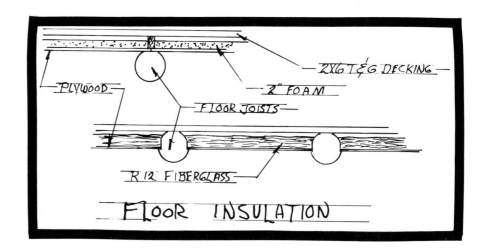

PLYWOOD

2X6 T&G DECKING

2" FOAM

FLOOR JOISTS

R 12 FIBERGLASS

FLOOR INSULATION

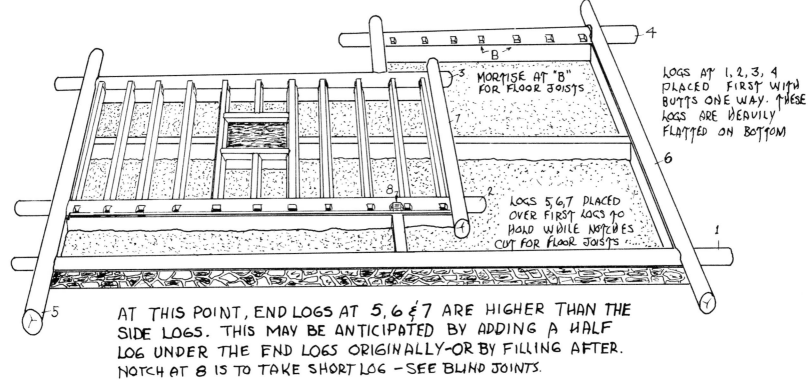

4

B

3 MORTISE AT "B" FOR FLOOR JOISTS

7

8

2

1

5

6

LOGS AT 1, 2, 3, 4 PLACED FIRST WITH BUTTS ONE WAY. THESE LOGS ARE HEAVILY FLATTED ON BOTTOM

LOGS 5, 6, 7 PLACED OVER FIRST LOGS TO HOLD WHILE NOTCHES CUT FOR FLOOR JOISTS

AT THIS POINT, END LOGS AT 5, 6 & 7 ARE HIGHER THAN THE SIDE LOGS. THIS MAY BE ANTICIPATED BY ADDING A HALF LOG UNDER THE END LOGS ORIGINALLY—OR BY FILLING AFTER. NOTCH AT 8 IS TO TAKE SHORT LOG —SEE BLIND JOINTS.

FIRST LOGS & FLOOR JOISTS

Hewing

In order to hew a log to serve as a floor joist, ceiling joist, or roof beam, it will be necessary to acquire a broad axe. No other axe will make the straight faced cut and smooth surface as well or as fast as the broad axe does. But because these are so difficult to obtain, I include here the dimensions so that a blacksmith can make one up. As mentioned under the heading of Tools, earlier, the broadaxe should be about 8 or 10 lbs. and should have a 36" offset helve.

A scoring axe is also used in hewing. This is a single bitted axe which will weigh 5 to 7 lbs. One or two log dogs will be handy, with an 8 lb. sledge to drive them and, if the timber is very large, splitting wedges will be useful. The chalk line will be needed, too.

Place the log in the desired position, probably on a short log under each end and dog it to the short log. Snap a chalk line where the cut is to be made. To make a chalk line, first, drive a small nail into the end of the log at the point where the hewing line is to originate (a), as

illustrated on the following page. Now stretch the line tightly to a second nail in a corresponding position (b) at the other end of the log. Loop one end of the chalk line around the nail (a), and tie securely at the other end of the log to the nail (b), letting the container hang freely. With the chalk line now stretched in line with the hewing surface, simply lift it up -- straight up -- at about midpoint, and let it snap smartly back into place. It will inflict a perfect line of powdered chalk where it strikes. This should give a readily visible line to hew. This, actually, is "hewing the line".

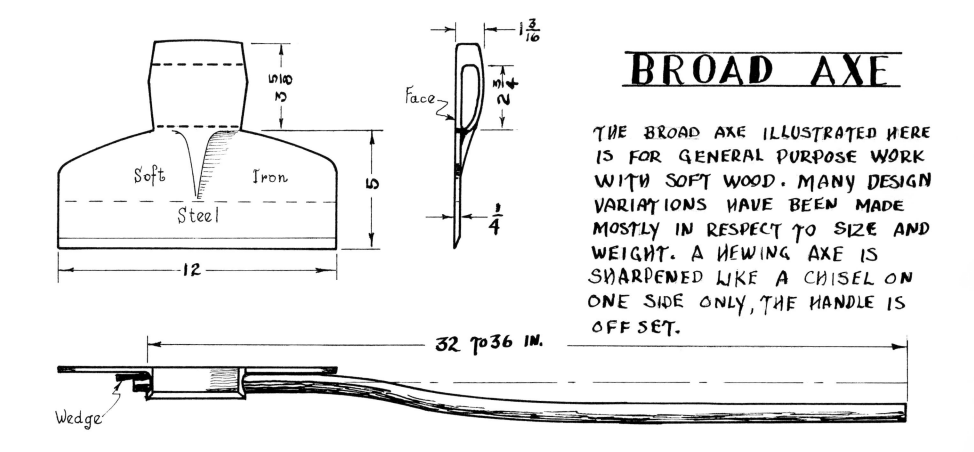

Soft   Iron

Steel

Face

BROAD AXE

THE BROAD AXE ILLUSTRATED HERE IS FOR GENERAL PURPOSE WORK WITH SOFT WOOD. MANY DESIGN VARIATIONS HAVE BEEN MADE MOSTLY IN RESPECT TO SIZE AND WEIGHT. A HEWING AXE IS SHARPENED LIKE A CHISEL ON ONE SIDE ONLY, THE HANDLE IS OFFSET.

Wedge

32 TO 36 IN.

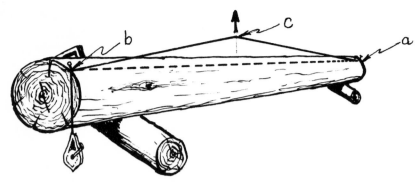

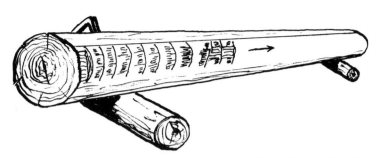

Chalk line stretched very tightly between nails (a) and (b), lifted straight up at (c), then allowed to snap down onto the log to print the cutting line.

Scoring partly done. Work forward to that chips will break free. Scoring cuts should be 6 to 8" apart and very nearly to the depth of the cutting line.

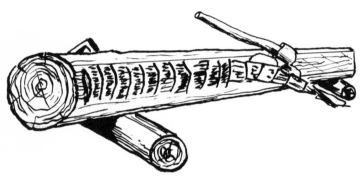

Final step . . . the slab is hewn from the log. With practice, a very fine finish may be obtained.

Large timbers can be hewn by first cutting the slab into sections and then splitting off the excess material.

While standing on the log, score cut as shown above, right, by chopping vertical cuts about 6 to 8" apart along the side of the log to the depth of the chalkline for the full length of the log.

Now the broad axe is used. Stepping back along the log as work progresses, use strong stokes that are nearly straight down, and slice off the slab according to the chalked line. If the timber is very big, cuts may be made to the chalked line every 3 or 4 feet and excess wood split off with wedges before finishing with the broad axe, as indicated .

Hewing requires a good eye, skill, and strength, and an admiration for the oldtime axemen is quickly learned. 50 railroad ties a day was the winter's average cut by one of the best tie hackers working near Burns Lake when the C.N.R. line was being built. They say he appeared to work very slowly. But each time his broad axe dropped, it took a 3 or 4 foot slab off the log. Ties were 8 feet long and 10" on the face and, at 17¢ apiece, the tie hackers seemed to make a living. An indication of their skill and strength was that the log bunk house for this tie camp at Priestley was erected in

one day by the 30 or 40 men waiting to get to work. Two fallers in the woods nearby skidded out the spruce logs with a team of horses to two men on the site who cut the horns off and sent the logs up to the 6 or 8 men on the building. Others packed moss, prepared the scoop roofing, or made bunks. "Next day they built the cookhouse," the camp boss told me. "They had to. The day after that, they wanted to start *work*." It saddens me that these men are so forgotten that sometimes, when I mention tie hackers, I see someone examining my necktie, lost in puzzlement.

Walls

The real work of building may now go forward . . . and here we will expect to use a round notch. I prefer this one for its simplicity and strength, its ability to shed water, and for the fact that the finished log still looks like a natural log. Suitable logs (generally the largest at the bottom) can now be rolled up onto the side walls of the building with the butt ends the opposite way to those of the first logs. These logs will rest on the end walls which are, of course, at right angles and higher.

Place the log accurately over the position it is expected finally to occupy and roll it until the optimum position for scribing has been obtained. That position will be one giving the straightest wall possible with the least amount of wood to be removed, while, at the same time, keeping at least part of the bow upwards. In this position, a preliminary scribe may be made at the notch to bring the log down part way when that notch is cut.

Most builders bring the new log down to within 1″ to 4″ of the log below, depending either upon their preference or upon the type of scribers they are using. Some people take the full scribe line from this initial position by blocking up one end of the log, if necessary, to obtain a uniform scribe and then carefully scribing the entire log. I would suggest that the builder should be well experienced before attempting this and in all probability, he will be better off to cut a preliminary notch that will give him his best scribing location for the log.

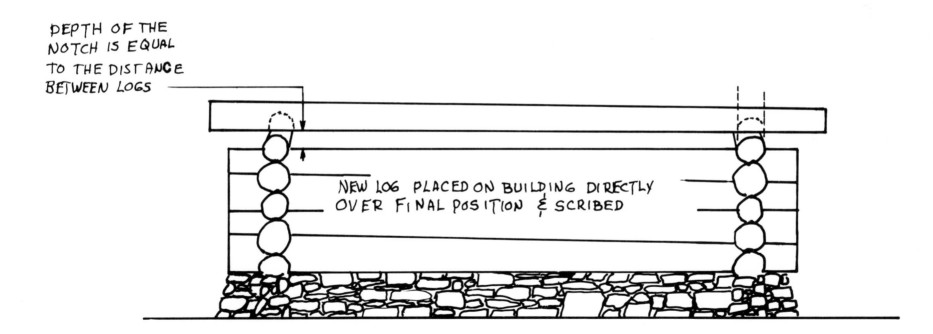

DEPTH OF THE NOTCH IS EQUAL TO THE DISTANCE BETWEEN LOGS

NEW LOG PLACED ON BUILDING DIRECTLY OVER FINAL POSITION & SCRIBED

CUTTING ROUND NOTCH

STEP.-1

The first cut with a chain saw or an axe will be straight down to the scribe line at centre. Step 3.

The second cuts should originate at the scribe line at the top (Step 4) and terminate at the scribe line near the bottom of the first cut. This will remove most of the wood from the notch. The remainder may be removed by means of several overlapping cuts along the side (Step 5) with a chain saw, which will give a stepped appearance or, with the axe, simply chopped out. In either case, be careful to stay within the boundaries of the scribed lines. The cut may be left in this condition, or smoothed out . . . as suits the builder.

When the log is turned down, it should present an even gap along its length so that the final scribe to bring it down to its intended location will remove as little wood as possible. Some additional trimming or blocking up may be required to accomplish this.

The final scribe, which would be taken at the widest gap, will require a notch depth ½ the diameter of the log . . . or as near to that as is possible.

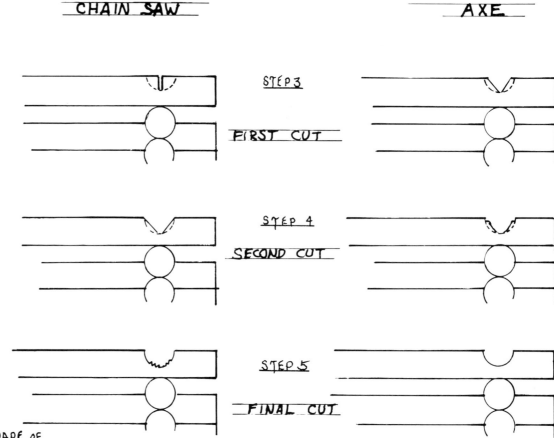

CHAIN SAW   AXE

STEP 3 — FIRST CUT

STEP 4 — SECOND CUT

STEP 5 — FINAL CUT

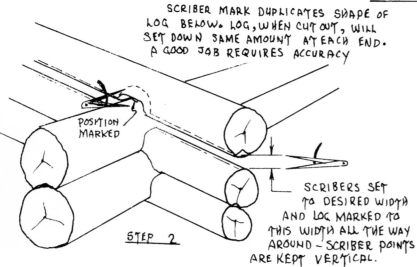

SCRIBER MARK DUPLICATES SHAPE OF LOG BELOW. LOG, WHEN CUT OUT, WILL SET DOWN SAME AMOUNT AT EACH END. A GOOD JOB REQUIRES ACCURACY

POSITION MARKED

STEP 2

SCRIBERS SET TO DESIRED WIDTH AND LOG MARKED TO THIS WIDTH ALL THE WAY AROUND – SCRIBER POINTS ARE KEPT VERTICAL.

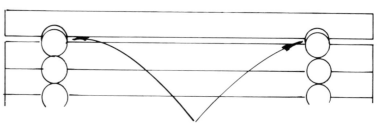

SCRIBE DISTANCE BETWEEN THESE POINTS SHOULD BE AS UNIFORM AS POSSIBLE TO PROVIDE A NARROW GROOVE

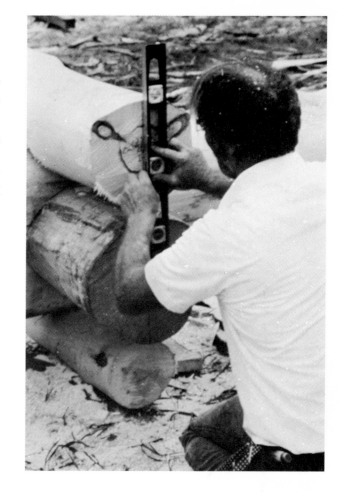

At this juncture, trim the log ends by bringing the length of the log below up with the level, as I am doing at left.

Cut the log ends off squarely, as illustrated, below left. Some people trim only every other log in order to leave some protruding ends to support scaffolding.

Next line up the log ends by placing a centre line plumb (photo at top right) on the end of the log you are working on and aligning this with the centre of the wall below. Note that the centre line on the log may have to be offset, if you are dealing with some difficult logs. The illustration at right below gives a simplified concept of lining up the centres.

Scribe the notches, the length of the log, and the ends, both inside and out. Make sure that the scribe line is complete because it is very difficult to replace the log in its original position, if it is once moved.

Take care that the log remains stationary until the scribe line is completed. The log may be bumped or someone may lean against it, causing a shift in position. If this occurs partway through a scribe, it results in error in the final fit.

TRIM TO LENGTH

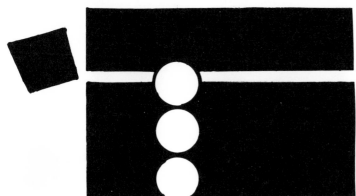

LINE UP CENTERS

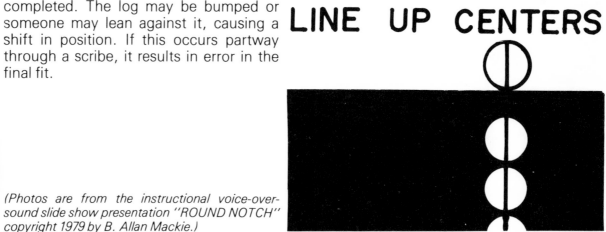

(Photos are from the instructional voice-over-sound slide show presentation "ROUND NOTCH" copyright 1979 by B. Allan Mackie.)

More about using scribers

The purpose of a pair of log scribers is to transfer a predetermined measurement directly from one surface to an adjacent surface with a high degree of faithfulness. In log work, this means the transferring of the pattern of the log below to the surface of the log above. Scribers may also be used for finishing work along floors, partitions, windows, and doors.

The scriber points are set to the widest space showing between two logs. The cutting points are kept vertical, that is, directly above one another and the handle is held in as perfect a horizontal position as you can manage . . . a feat made easier

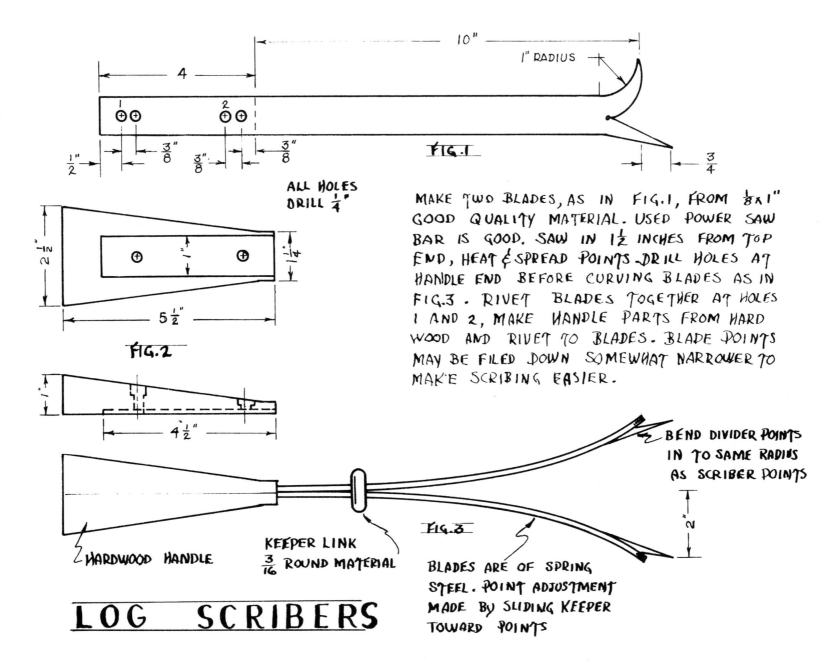

FIG.1

ALL HOLES DRILL ¼"

FIG.2

MAKE TWO BLADES, AS IN FIG.1, FROM ⅛ x 1" GOOD QUALITY MATERIAL. USED POWER SAW BAR IS GOOD. SAW IN 1½ INCHES FROM TOP END, HEAT & SPREAD POINTS. DRILL HOLES AT HANDLE END BEFORE CURVING BLADES AS IN FIG.3. RIVET BLADES TOGETHER AT HOLES 1 AND 2, MAKE HANDLE PARTS FROM HARD WOOD AND RIVET TO BLADES. BLADE POINTS MAY BE FILED DOWN SOMEWHAT NARROWER TO MAKE SCRIBING EASIER.

BEND DIVIDER POINTS IN TO SAME RADIUS AS SCRIBER POINTS

HARDWOOD HANDLE

KEEPER LINK ³⁄₁₆ ROUND MATERIAL

FIG.3

BLADES ARE OF SPRING STEEL. POINT ADJUSTMENT MADE BY SLIDING KEEPER TOWARD POINTS

LOG SCRIBERS

if there is a level mounted directly on the scriber. The scribed line is carried up over the notch, in the case of a round notch (a, Figure 5) and on to the end of the log (b, Fig. 5) that extends past the wall. Scribe both the inside and the outside of the log. Use the divider ends for marking around the notch because the hooked points of a scratch scriber will not function here.

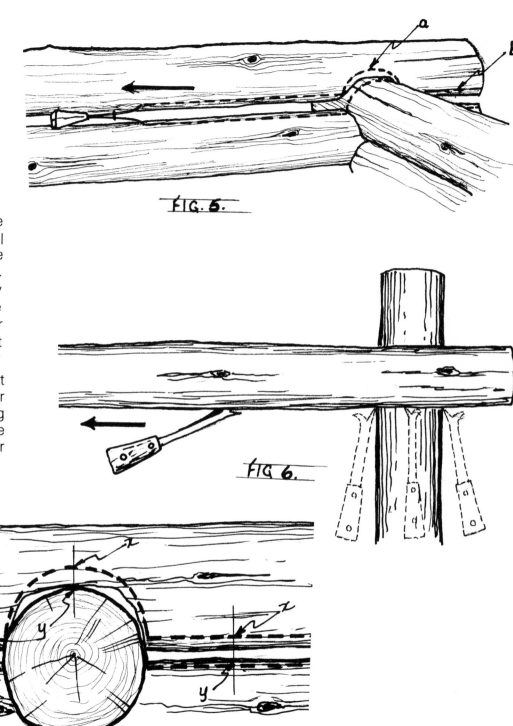

FIG. 5.

FIG. 6.

FIG 7.

The whole idea of scribing is that the two lines so formed are a constant vertical distance apart at any two points, one above the other (x, y of Figure 7). Therefore, by cutting away the intervening wood on the upper log, it must drop to an exact fit on the log below

Careful work can create a fit that requires little insulation. It should never require "chinking" in the usual meaning of that word, i.e., the application of some substance or material to the wall after construction. Nor do I ever use the term "chinkless" since -- like cabin -- the word has no place within the context of a 20th century standard of construction.

FIG. 4.

The scribing of a log might take the beginner as much as an hour's time to complete, but it is time well spent.

When the marking has been completed, the log should be rolled inward on the building so that the notches are up, for the finishing work to be done. Always when turning the log back up, roll it inward, toward the centre of the building, since this is much safer.

If the notch is to be finished with a chain saw, first score around the scribe line with a short-bladed knife or a chisel. This will prevent the fraying of the wood

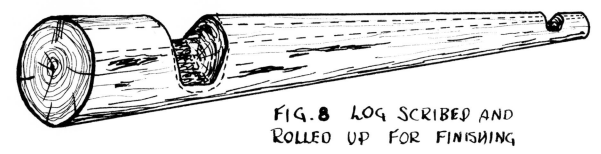

FIG. 8 LOG SCRIBED AND ROLLED UP FOR FINISHING

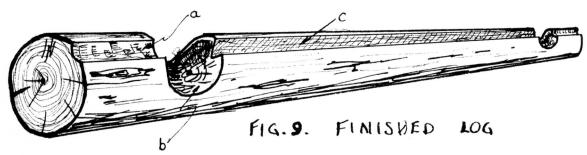

FIG. 9. FINISHED LOG

The included angle of this cut should be about 80°. If this work has been done well, no further dressing or fitting is required.

The end or extension portion of the log -- that part on the outside of the notch -- should have a cove-shaped groove for its entire length. It is a mistake to cut a V-groove here and simply cove out the last few inches, because subsequent trimming of the logs ends may expose the V-cut and the work will depreciate in appearance.

With practice, a perfect fit may be obtained almost every time. In this regard, I would like to emphasize that a narrow groove is tighter, stronger, and much quicker to do than is a wide lateral groove.

at the edges of the notch. Work only on the side of the log near your so that you can see the line that you're working to.

Cut down to the scribe line at the centre slightly more than halfway across the notch and with a very slight tilt into the cut. Then widen this cut by making overlapping cuts to the depth of the scribe line, working ¼ at a time. When all four quarters have been completed, you should have a notch that is smooth, sharp to the edge, and very slightly concave in the centre (¼" to ½" low in the centre). Some people, to obtain an easier and more perfect appearing notch, tend to hollow out far too much . . . this leaves a thin wall on the log that is not able to support the weight it should. Consequently, as the notch-edge is crushed, a disproportionate amount of weight is transferred to the wall length which may result in a log being forced out of position. If this happens it is virtually impossible to repair. So it is best to be sure that the notch edges are strong.

A two-stage cut is probably best, when making the long groove down the length of the log between the notches...the lateral groove. First make a shallow cut ½" to ¾" deep that follows just inside the scribe line and is aimed at the diameter of the log. The second cut is made at a shallower angle and uses the first cut for a guide.

Lateral groove: the chain saw is following a scribed line.

Preceeding Photos: *Scriber points (set to the widest space between the two rough-notched logs) must at all times be kept vertical, the handle* *in the horizontal position. Here a student, using my scribers, draws the scribed line around the notch with the scriber ends, the long wall line with* *the hooked points.* **Above:** *This perfectly fitted round notch could not have been achieved without strict attention to scribing.*

More about walls

A good looking building must have walls that are straight and plumb. But

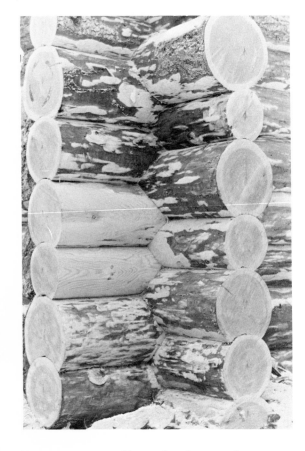

logs are not uniform in size or shape, nor are they always entirely straight. A workable method is necessary, therefore, to achieve properly aligned walls. Apart from appearance, it is important that the weight should bear as nearly straight down as possible so as to prevent any log from springing or settling out of place.

Decide first whether you wish to line up the inside or the outside of the walls, or whether to line up the centres of the logs. I think that lining up the centres assures that the weight is better balanced and

gives a natural appearance on both sides of the walls.

One method of aligning a wall on the centres is to use a plumb or carpenter's level on every second log at the butt end, placing the centre of the top log directly over the centre of the butt directly below it. This gives reasonable results if the material is uniform in size.

A better method is to erect a straight pole or a 2x4 as a sight (see photo below and Fig. 1 on following page). This sighting pole may be placed at one end of each wall, a convenient distance from the building … perhaps 20 feet away to be out of the main activity. If the log to be aligned is rough notched and in place near its final position, it will be possible to sight the centre line of the log from a position beyond the end of the wall and slightly above it. It should be possible to judge this log in relation to the real centre line and in respect to the general development of the wall. For instance, if a log has a slight sweep to the outside, much can be done to even out the general appearance by moving its two ends slightly inward, sometimes only ½" will do the job.

A bulged wall is probably one of the most common errors in misalignment. This is a wall that creeps outward as the building goes up, then creeps back in when the correction is attempted. Structurally this is bad even if the top log ends up directly over the first log. It is better to be ruthless and make the required correction as soon as the deviation is noted. It will look better in the long run and will be more stable.

Sometimes, in order to use a log which might otherwise be too short, it is possible to cut through at window and door openings, and extend the length. This would mean that two or three short logs are to be used instead of one … an economical trick if the log supply is running low, too, as some discarded butts and tops might be put to use. Have all the short lengths in line at once, and scribe them all, just as if it were one log. Balance them on the building by nailing a board onto the window or door-opening and, of course, also nailed to the end of the short log. These short lengths might have to be taken down off the building in order for the notch and groove to be cut but if this

LINING UP WALLS

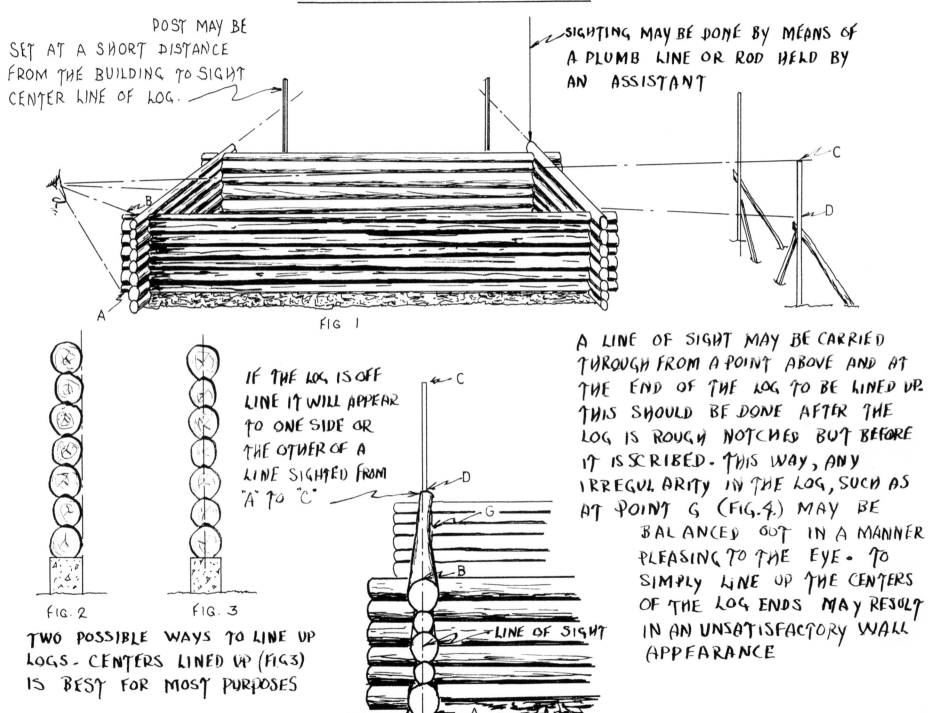

POST MAY BE SET AT A SHORT DISTANCE FROM THE BUILDING TO SIGHT CENTER LINE OF LOG.

SIGHTING MAY BE DONE BY MEANS OF A PLUMB LINE OR ROD HELD BY AN ASSISTANT

FIG 1

IF THE LOG IS OFF LINE IT WILL APPEAR TO ONE SIDE OR THE OTHER OF A LINE SIGHTED FROM "A" TO "C"

FIG. 2

FIG. 3

TWO POSSIBLE WAYS TO LINE UP LOGS. CENTERS LINED UP (FIG 3) IS BEST FOR MOST PURPOSES

LINE OF SIGHT

FIG 4

A LINE OF SIGHT MAY BE CARRIED THROUGH FROM A POINT ABOVE AND AT THE END OF THE LOG TO BE LINED UP. THIS SHOULD BE DONE AFTER THE LOG IS ROUGH NOTCHED BUT BEFORE IT IS SCRIBED. THIS WAY, ANY IRREGULARITY IN THE LOG, SUCH AS AT POINT G (FIG. 4) MAY BE BALANCED OUT IN A MANNER PLEASING TO THE EYE. TO SIMPLY LINE UP THE CENTERS OF THE LOG ENDS MAY RESULT IN AN UNSATISFACTORY WALL APPEARANCE is not convenient use a scaffold or bench to roll them aside (into the building rather than offside).

Permit the log ends to run well beyond the corners, to provide a greater choice of style in finishing them. Never cut closer than 8 or 10 inches from the wall.

Note that, for a carefully finished log end, the groove should not be carried beyond the corners. Instead, the outer extremity of the log ends are scribed to fit exactly the contour of the log below -- scooped, rather than channelled -- to fit as tightly together as possible.

Sealing between the logs

In the olden days, log buildings often were put up with the intention of driving

some material into the seams between the logs at some later date. But this kind of "chinking" which can be driven in, can also fall out, and it usually did. Another school of thought was that no attempt should be made to bring the logs tightly together but, rather, split wood strips or slim poles could be nailed over these many breezeways. It created a lot more work and it detracted from the appearance of the logs.

My own method, until the last few years, was to cut a V-shaped groove the length of the log and to stuff it with sphagnum moss if it were available, or with fibreglass if it were not. The "V" has now become flatter with a double cut or is coved when done by hand. The stuffing was done by driving wedges between the logs after 3 rounds were up, packing the moss in lightly and evenly, then knocking the wedges out to clamp the "V" tightly down over the moss. This procedure gives a permanent, bug-proof, organic, free, and airtight fit.

I recommend the use of moss whenever possible. It has some qualities which remain, in my estimation, unsurpassed by any of the products of technology. Use sphagnum moss, the variety that grows in the shade of spruce or pine, where the snow melts last of all in spring.

Good moss forms a blanket about 4 to 6 inches deep with only a few wood lilies or lady slippers growing through. The top layer will be pale green, but underneath it turns to brown. All of it can be used as it will most likely peel clean from the ground. If weather permits, an expedition should be planned for collecting the moss, for not only is this a good place for a picnic with blueberries nearby at the

right time of year, but also, a great deal of moss is required for even a small building. So the whole family can be pleasantly busy for most of a day stuffing moss into sacks.

Moss can be gathered far in advance and stored in sacks, as it stays in good condition almost indefinitely. Fresh moss is handled more easily than dried-out moss which becomes brittle. Plastic bags tied at the top will retain the moisture but if for any reason the moss does become dry before it is used, a light sprinkling of water restores it to its former flexibility immediately. The moss dries again quickly, once it is stuffed into the walls, but I find the dampness desirable as it causes the moss to form itself more perfectly to the contours of the logs.

Participants in my log building classes have expressed more skepticism toward the use of moss than toward any other aspect of log building, including my positive dislike of mechanically peeled logs and indoor toilets. One expert builder confided in me that his wife would never permit him to use moss in her home as she was a very clean woman. Up to that point, I had never been aware of any cause to question my wife's attitude toward sanitation and considering my uninterrupted good health for the past twenty-six years of marriage, I feel that the implication is not valid. For moss to have been used as a bandage for wounds, the material has to be exceptionally clean. "But doesn't moss attract mice and bugs?" they persist. Perhaps so, but I have never seen them. I did, however, find a newborn family of mice in a batt of fibreglass which had been left at the building project by a student wishing tactfully to introduce me to this material. By placing some heavy logs around the fibreglass I was able to protect the rodents from accident or injury so that, in due course, I had the satisfaction of observing 8 mice emerge from their pink fibreglass nursery in an excellent state of health. They were, I admit, extremely clean young mice. As yet, I have found no sample of a moss mouse nursery by which a comparison could have been made. So far as I know, mice and bugs do not live in moss.

I have become so curious about this widespread skepticism toward moss that I have made a point of examining old and roofless log buildings and, in spite of the obvious soakings and resulting rot, I have found no sign of insect association with the moss. This surprised even me, for I understood that insects, given moisture, could live in almost any forest substance. Another surprise was to note the state of preservation in the wood surrounding the compressed moss; it was firmer than the wood in the rest of the log. Therefore, my opinion of the value of moss has simply increased. I can only guess that skepticism is actually a lack of confidence due to the unfamiliarity of moss as a building material. This, and the fact that it is free. I can't say I actually understand this, any more than I understand why fiddlehead fern and mushrooms go to waste in the woods while people buy these things all faded and frozen and at high cost from a store.

This is not to suggest that fibreglass is not a good material. I use it frequently in logwork when it is not possible to obtain moss. And I use it in floor and roof insulation, of course. But I do believe that manufactured building materials should be avoided when a free and equally good fibre is available. So I will simply note here that I have seen moss used successfully as floor insulation too.

It should, however, be noted that if a wide "V" is cut in a log, there is a tendency for this log to hang up on knots or any other irregularity at the shoulder. This will cause a separation between the logs and the moss, with consequent leakage or draughts of air, as shown at (a). Of

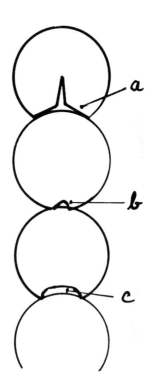

course, the same result will be evident if fibreglass insulation is used. The remedy -- or prevention -- is to cut a narrow groove so that the weight of the log bears along the sharp edge of the groove (b). On occasion, a wide groove may be unavoidable; in which case, cove out the groove (c) so that a close shoulder does not interfere.

Other notches

Many types of corners have been developed and tried, either out of tradition or to fill a particular need. Several of the more common types are illustrated on the following pages. The saddle notch is favoured because it is strong and sheds water effectively. This notch can be used with round logs drawn down and grooved to give a tight fit for their full length. The **saddle notch** must be carefully fitted to avoid an amateurish appearance. A **locked joint** or "**egg crate**" joint is easily made and gives a good appearance. It is strong and stable, well suited to hewn timbers. The log ends may be left long to give a more casual appearance. A drawback to this style is, however, that it would be very difficult to groove the logs for the tight fit which is so important to the thermal resistance values of the building. The **Hudson's Bay corner** must surely have been misnamed. It is formed by spiking the logs to boxed upright planks at the corners. It is unstable and does not allow the logs to settle firmly together. Certainly it has no similarity to the strength and workmanship of actual Hudson's Bay Company buildings. It is possibly a name given to those who built rapidly, to be close to the HBC post. It may be a regional misnomer. But it is not at all suitable for anyone wishing to draw and groove the logs to a tight fit. **Lapped corners** are easily and quickly done and may even be done with a saw or chain saw so that these are generally used where speed is important. While the drawn fit could be accomplished, the extra time required to recut the corner might just as well be spent making a dovetail corner which would be stronger

and more securely locked. The **dovetail corner** seems to be a natural outgrowth of a lapped corner. By simply changing the angle of the cuts slightly so that they slope inward, a naturally locked joint is formed. For complete information on the subject of notches, please refer to NOTCHES OF ALL KINDS.

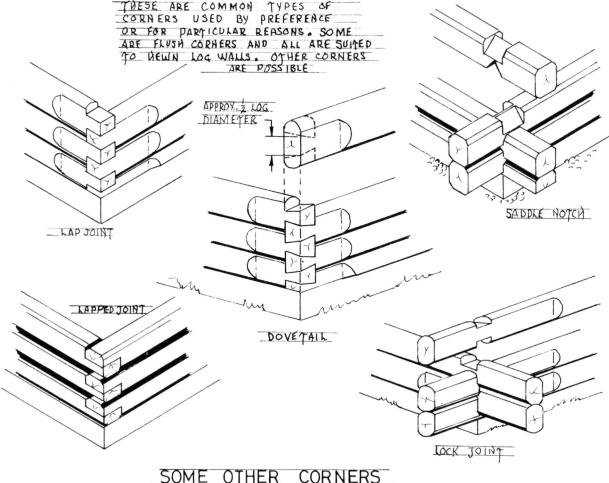

THESE ARE COMMON TYPES OF CORNERS USED BY PREFERENCE OR FOR PARTICULAR REASONS. SOME ARE FLUSH CORNERS AND ALL ARE SUITED TO HEWN LOG WALLS. OTHER CORNERS ARE POSSIBLE

LAP JOINT

APPROX. ½ LOG DIAMETER

SADDLE NOTCH

LAPPED JOINT

DOVETAIL

LOCK JOINT

SOME OTHER CORNERS

More about Dovetail Corners

These are considered by many to be the ultimate in log building construction and, from certain points of view, this opinion is well justified. In other words, there are pitfalls to consider before taking the final decision to use a dovetail corner.

First, it is necessary to have very high quality timber to make a good job of this corner, particulary if the log is to be hewn flat. If the timber is given to excessive taper, the hewn face will run out to round and a less pleasing appearance will result. Indeed, sometimes it has proven impossible to lower a log to meet the one below because the top end was too small. This leaves a gap in the wall which must be filled effectively if a warm building is to be hoped for.

Second, the logs must be straight grained and not given to compression wood because if the tree has grown on an exposed site which produces these qualities, the log may twist in its carefully and laboriously fitted position, destroying much of the effectiveness of the joint, not to mention the appearance of the work.

Third, much judgment is required to produce a satisfying job and this may be one of the main reasons why an expert axeman may choose this style. Certainly, it is a challenge to the skill and judgment of even a practised builder.

But there is a great deal to recommend the dovetail corner. It is strong, stable, and will stand square and true longer than most. It sheds water well and, assuming that the timber is large, creates a tight and weatherproof fit. So for those who prefer this style of construction, the following is intended as a guide. If this style is to be attempted for the first time, I would recommend the construction of a small building first, by way of practice and experience. Or, at the very least, a few experimental corners.

To begin, select a wall thickness which can be accomplished by all the logs (Fig. 1, A) that are to be included in the walls. This measurement will be about ⅔ to ¾ of the diameter of the smallest log at the small end, in order to produce a suitable

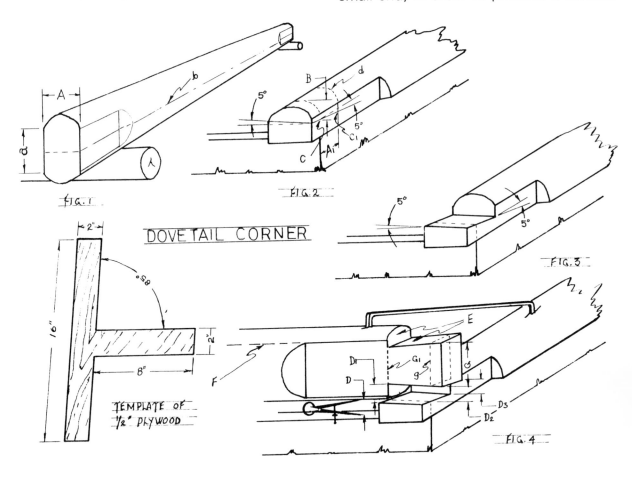

DOVETAIL CORNER

face width "a", Fig. 1. Suitable measurements usually range from 6″ to 8″ but thicker walls may well be considered. For a 6″ wall, the smallest top diameter should be about 8″. Smaller logs have certainly been used but the skill required to place them becomes increasingly demanding.

The log to be shaped should be blocked up at each end so that it will belly down, and the ends hewn for a distance of about 12″ to 18″ to the wall thickness selected (A, Fig. 1). Care must be taken that the ends are made straight and true. Now the log is turned so that the flatted ends rest on the blocks in a horizontal position. By means of a chalk line, a centre line may be marked on the log ('b', Fig. 1) and the log split in half with a chain saw, one half to be used on each end of the building. If the walls are to rest on corner blocks only, then of course this is not necessary; use the full log. If the log is not sufficiently large or if a chain saw is not used, then the log may be flattened down with a broad axe.

Place a log on the foundation wall at each end of the building. Then place a mark equal to the wall thickness back toward the centre from each end mark (C1, Fig. 2). Next, locate a point on the outside face of the log, directly above the corner, which is ¼ of the log diameter down from the top of the log (B, Fig. 2). From this point, slope a line downward at about 5° from level and toward the centre of the log to intersect the vertical line marking the width of the wall (C to C1, Fig. 2). With a sharp handsaw, make the vertical cut (d, Fig. 2). The bottom of this cut will slope up 5° from point C1 (lines may be extended to the end of the log to assist in obtaining an accurate cut and, in any case, some extra length should be left on the log). Lastly, flatten this surface. The finished surface should slant 5° from the horizontal both toward the centre of the log and toward the outside edge. (Fig. 3).

When all four corners of the building have been treated in this manner and the first two logs are on the building **with the butt ends the same way,** the side logs are ready to be placed with both their butt ends pointed in the same direction (the second full round will have the butts at opposite ends, that is, the two butt ends meeting the two top ends on the one side, and two butts coming down on two tops on the other side). These logs may be cut slightly longer than the wall and flattened at the ends to wall width while still on the ground if there is some mechanical means of raising them onto the building. If the logs are to be rolled up onto the walls, however, it is perhaps better to do this work on the building.

When the ends have been flattened, turn the log belly up and in the exact position relative to the final position it is to occupy (Fig. 4) and secure it in place with a log dog. The hewn face must be truly vertical. By means of a pair of dividers, determine the distance the log is to be lowered (at each end) to meet the foundation (D, Fig. 4). Carefully transfer this measurement to the positions D1, D2, D3, and D4 (on the inside corner) and join these points with a pencil line on the hewn face of the log (for example, D1 to D2 and D3 to D4). When this has been done on each end of the log, the log may be turned over and the cut made. If the layout has been done with accuracy, the corner will show an excellent fit. Slight irregularities can be corrected by slipping the tip of a hand saw into the joint and working off any excess wood.

When the log is resting in place, the top cuts may be made (E. Fig. 4). Draw a plumb line ("g", Fig. 4) on the outside of the log and measure back the wall width (G1). Mark off about ½ the log diameter on this outside corner (G) then mark off the sloped line. To obtain uniformity in this, a template, as illustrated in Fig. 5, will be useful.

When all four corners have been prepared, the second round of logs can be started. If a closer fit through the length of the log is desired, ½ to ¾″ extra width should be set on the dividers at D (Fig. 3) and when the log is turned into place, a template of this thickness will be placed under each end -- the same at each end. Now set the scribers to the width of the template and scribe the length of the log. The log may now be "scooped" to this line to obtain the tight fit that keeps a building warm. Some people advocate running a power saw back and forth between the logs to accomplish this fit but I find this a crude and inaccurate method, particulary when the saw is in inexpert hands.

If the builder wishes to hew the logs flat for their full length, either inside or out or both, now is the time to do it. A chalk line may be snapped onto the top of the log between the flattened ends (F, Fig. 4). The single plane wall surface obtained this way is suited to a building constructed of large logs. Many solid and beautiful examples of hewn log buildings still exist in British Columbia, some of which are 150 years old. Shown here is the main trading post of the Hudson's Bay Company at Fort St. James, constructed in the French method of pièce-en-pièce. The meat cache is done in the same style. I include here a glimpse of a roof at Batoche, Sask., the only other example I have seen of this way of finishing the eaves. Of historical interest is the fact that the original trading post and meat cache were built under the North West Co. fur traders from Montreal, of which Alexander Mackenzie and Simon Fraser were partners. In 1821 when the Hudson's Bay Co. absorbed the Nor'Westers, a clerk's house was added to the Fort St. James establishment and this building (dovetail corner pictured on page 52) was built by a Scot using quite a different style. All three of the remaining structures are in remarkably good repair considering the lack of concern shown by governments toward what was once the chief fur trading post in New Caledonia and the onetime residence of James Douglas who was later to become British Columbia's first Governor.

Pièce-en-pièce construction

Pièce-en-pièce construction is an old and honourable method of building in Canada. It is closely related to timber framing and as such is a direct ancestor of modern platform framing.

The main advantage of this type of construction is that it makes it possible to construct very large buildings with relatively short logs.

The timbers were usually hewn or sawn square, although round logs can be used equally well. The vertical members are slotted to hold the tongues at each end of the horizontal logs.

A good foundation is of the utmost importance, as is the settling space above the horizontal members, because of the uneven settling which is bound to occur.

Pièce-en-pièce building at Jasper Park Lodge, Alberta.

The original trading post at Fort St. James, on Stuart Lake, built in 1806 by the North West Co. of Montreal, later the main Hudson's Bay post in B.C.

The meat cache at H.B.C. post, Fort St. James.

At Batoche, Saskatchewan, overlooking the battlefield of the 2nd Riel rebellion.

For further information on pièce en pièce construction, see THE CANADIAN LOG HOUSE No. 2 (1975) p. 46, and NOTCHES OF ALL KINDS, A Book of Timber Joinery.

Putting the logs up on the building

When the building is two or three rounds high, it becomes more difficult to get the logs up onto the walls. A crane or a fork lift is a luxury not usually found in the lone woodsman's tool cache and besides these machines create more mess in one day than a family can readily repair in a year. I prefer the method of rolling logs up on skids with one or two ropes, where the site is open and level enough. Where the site is steep, or in a situation where the logs cannot be dumped close to the building, it is possible to use an aspect of high lead logging.

Skids, shown below, are so simple a device as to need little description. On a low building, only short poles are needed to form the inclined plane on which to roll the logs. They should form an angle of about 30° to the horizontal and, of course, need not be too heavy. When the walls get high, however, tough and dry spruce poles will be easier to move. Have two sets of skids to avoid having to move them from one wall to another. A small notch in the end of the log on which the skids rest will hold it against rolling off to the side. The skid should not protrude much above the wall and may be cut at an angle to assist in keeping it low.

A rope is tied to the building at some opening or a peavey hook may be used for the anchor for the dead end. The rope is then passed under the log to be rolled up (see illustrations for Placing Logs) and over the building to the power source. In

Peavey hook used as a rope anchor.

the case of a small building, power may be supplied by several men or by a block and tackle. For larger buildings, you may need a horse, a tractor, or a truck. Nylon or polypropylene rope is very good, 3/8" cable is good, but Manila rope is adequate only for very small buildings.

As the log will roll faster at the butt end, this end should be placed lower on the skids (as a student and I are doing in the photo at left) so that both ends reach the top of the skids at the same time. Just before the log goes over the top end of the skids, a little additional speed will help prevent the log from slipping. It can readily be seen that a few extra feet of log length makes it much easier to keep control of the logs even if they do get a bit out of line. If it is raining, or if the logs are slippery, it will be necessay to have a rope at each end. The direction of the line pull can be changed by anchoring a pulley block near the centre of the building.

All parallel logs in a round can be pulled up in sequence, starting with the log for the far side of the building. This way it is possible to pull up logs on two sides of the building only, rather than from four sides. Logs may also be rolled up on only one side and turned on the building. This is sometimes desirable in order to make use of a difficult site or to preserve standing trees.

Placing logs

Walls are up and two logs have been placed on the gable end. Top logs & purlins are run out long in front to form roof support for porch. One wall opening has been roughly cut to make access easier. Rope is used to parbuckle log up. Two ropes might be used. Rope is placed off center to the butt of the log. Note that notches for purlins are now on top of the log so that end of gable log will not be cut off when roof slope is cut. Position of purlins is judged by using a straight edge from the wall at the desired pitch.

To turn a log on a building, roll it a few feet onto the walls and then drive an axe solidly into the log on which it is rolling (see illustration at right) on the side near the wall, so that when the other end of the log is rolled back it will butt up against the axehead. The log will now be across the corner of the building and may be brought around to right angles by judicious maneouvers. The log may be moved endwise by driving the peavey hook into it back of the wall on which the log is resting. Place the point of the peavey over the wall and "jack" the log ahead. This is very slow and is used only for small adjustments of a few inches. Or a log can be bounced over by rocking the log away from you and placing the corner of the axe under the log and prying ahead as the log rolls back.

"CUTTING" A LOG BACK TO TURN IT.

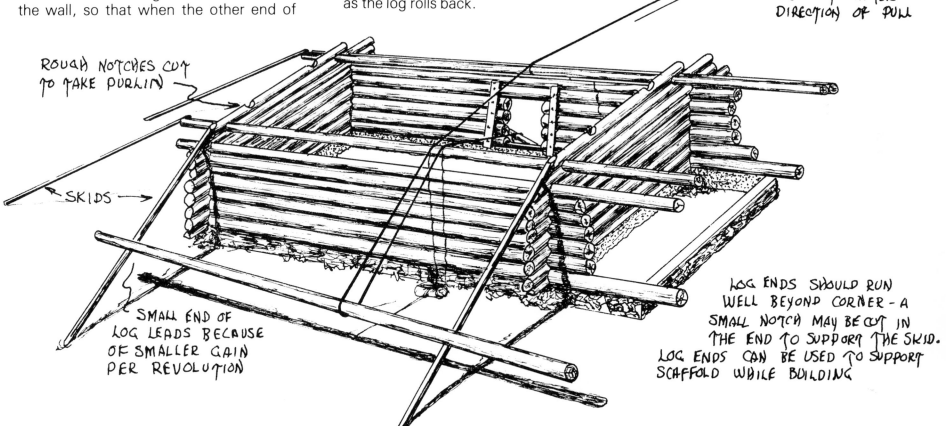

POWER SOURCE — BLOCK MAY BE USED TO ALTER DIRECTION OF PULL

ROUGH NOTCHES CUT TO TAKE PURLIN

SKIDS

SMALL END OF LOG LEADS BECAUSE OF SMALLER GAIN PER REVOLUTION

LOG ENDS SHOULD RUN WELL BEYOND CORNER - A SMALL NOTCH MAY BE CUT IN THE END TO SUPPORT THE SKID. LOG ENDS CAN BE USED TO SUPPORT SCAFFOLD WHILE BUILDING

High lead logging, as the builder will use it, borrows only those ideas and materials needed to lift logs from the ground onto his building. Actual high lead setups will not be described as their many systems of cables, blocks, and spar trees are used to accomplish much more complicated purposes than we need here. The term "high lead" explains the difference between having the "pull" exerted on the log from a source on the ground as opposed to having the pull exerted from a point above the log. In other words, lifting and swinging the log rather than dragging it. This difference explains why, when the site is a difficult one, it becomes desirable to be able to hoist the log clear of obstacles and set it on the building by remote control. The method suited here is the Skyline Carriage which, for practical purposes, should be limited to 100 to 200 feet. It consists of stretching a cable between two points so that the cable passes over the building site and the log pile or somewhere close to the log pile. The anchor points are most often good trees although A-frames, spar trees, or high ground would be suitable.

This method of placing logs on the building enables one man to work alone. It is well suited to doing the log fitting in one location and moving the logs, after they are shaped, to the building site.

5/8" steel core cable is suitable for moving most building logs for a distance of 200 feet but any error on the side of additional strength is a good idea. Cable ends should have eye splices in them. Cable clamps are not too suitable but can be used if there is no one around who can splice cable. Cables should be fastened to trees with a short "tree strap", which is a short piece of cable at least as large in diameter as the one which will be fastened to it, and it will have an eye splice in each end. One end is placed around the tree and the other slipped through it so that the tree is "choked". Other gear such as mainline blocks or skyline is shackled to the protruding eye. If a line is to be passed around a tree and shackled back on itself be sure that the shackle pin is in the eye rather than on the line so that working the line will not tend to screw the pin out. Logging spars require 6 guylines but for our purposes 2 should be enough unless there is to be a great deal of side pull. 3/8 or 1/2" rope core line is suitable for the illustrated setup. The line used to lift the logs is 3/4" nylon or polypropylene rope.

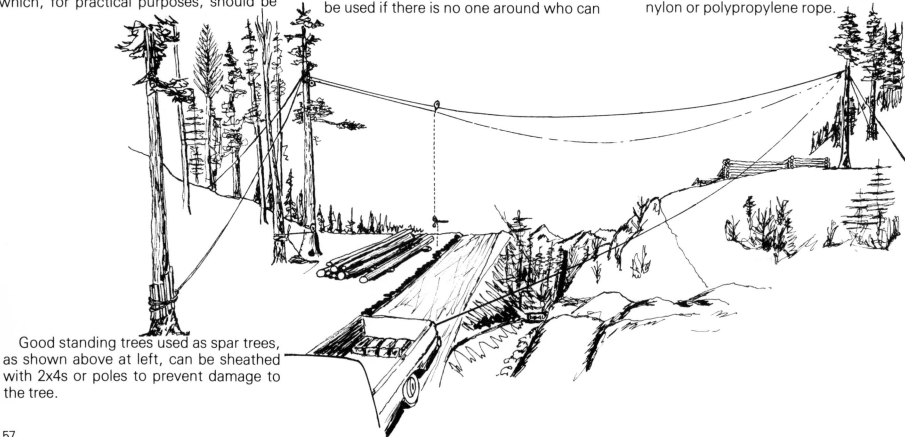

Good standing trees used as spar trees, as shown above at left, can be sheathed with 2x4s or poles to prevent damage to the tree.

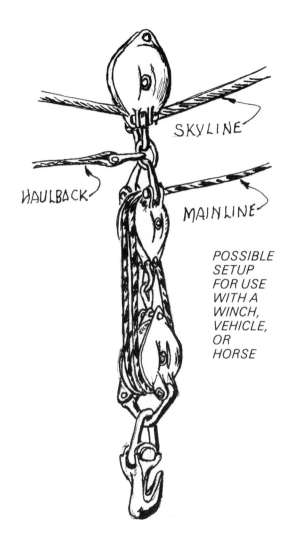

SKYLINE

HAULBACK

MAINLINE

POSSIBLE
SETUP
FOR USE
WITH A
WINCH,
VEHICLE,
OR
HORSE

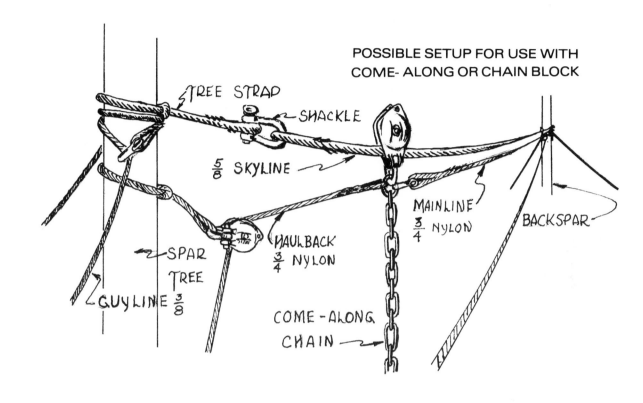

POSSIBLE SETUP FOR USE WITH
COME- ALONG OR CHAIN BLOCK

TREE STRAP

SHACKLE

$\frac{5}{8}$ SKYLINE

SPAR
TREE

GUYLINE $\frac{3}{8}$

HAULBACK
$\frac{3}{4}$ NYLON

MAINLINE
$\frac{3}{4}$ NYLON

BACKSPAR

COME - ALONG
CHAIN

Guylines should be choked to the spar tree as close as possible to the tree strap supporting the skyline. At the lower end, they may be secured to stumps, trees, or anchors buried in the ground. The main thing is to ensure that they are solid. For this kind of set up, three guylines would be an adequate number.

Framing the openings

When the log which will house the top of the doors and windows is in place (at about 7 ft. 0 inches above the floor), draw the final dimensions on both sides of it, then roll it back up and make the cuts. The log is much easier to work, in this position, and the work can be done better

and more safely, too. At the same time the keyways for the opening can be cut much more safely and conveniently than when the header log has been replaced.

If, at any time, a log does not align well with the centre line of the logs already in place, then at either a window or door opening, the offending log may be cut,

with some additional length allowance left intact for a final trim. In this way, the log can be brought into better alignment before it is scribed. This also gives a better appearance to the opening, makes framing easier, as well as straightening a crooked log or stretching a short one. The same technique may be applied to window openings.

Photo top left: short log lengths were used on either side of a window opening. Keyway is cut, but header log is not yet turned back and shaped. Lower left: in this pre-built roof, a window opening has been cut in the log gable end with ample settling space already prepared in the header log. Above right: a neat trim board covering the settling space gives a tidy appearance.

Settling allowance

Walls constructed of green logs will settle about ¾'' per foot of wall height. In effect, this means that door and window openings will reduce in size in proportion to their height (but not their width), as will walls, gable ends, stair wells, or any other portion of the building. Nor does the use of dry logs eliminate this tendency since settling will still occur due to the tightening of the log work; the factor may, however, be reduced for dry logs by approximately one half, to become 3/8'' per foot of wall.

Settling allowances must, therefore, be made at all points where vertical forces exist. The most frequent locations for settling problems involve doors, windows, roof support and masonry. Any

FRAMING OF OPENINGS

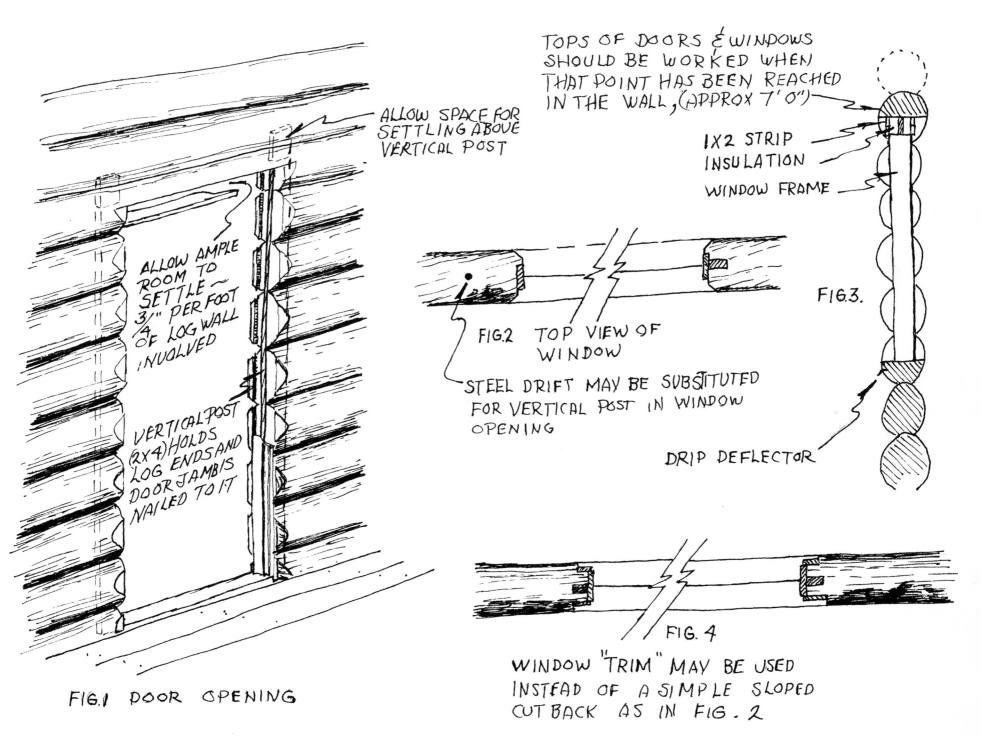

ALLOW SPACE FOR
SETTLING ABOVE
VERTICAL POST

TOPS OF DOORS & WINDOWS
SHOULD BE WORKED WHEN
THAT POINT HAS BEEN REACHED
IN THE WALL, (APPROX 7'0")

1X2 STRIP
INSULATION

WINDOW FRAME

ALLOW AMPLE
ROOM TO
SETTLE ~
3/4" PER FOOT
OF LOG WALL
INVOLVED

VERTICAL POST
(2X4) HOLDS
LOG ENDS AND
DOOR JAMB IS
NAILED TO IT

FIG. 3.

FIG. 2   TOP VIEW OF
WINDOW

STEEL DRIFT MAY BE SUBSTITUTED
FOR VERTICAL POST IN WINDOW
OPENING

DRIP DEFLECTOR

FIG. 4

FIG. 1 DOOR OPENING

WINDOW "TRIM" MAY BE USED
INSTEAD OF A SIMPLE SLOPED
CUT BACK AS IN FIG. 2

vertical support must be reduced in height to permit settling.

Settling is indeed a possible problem in a log building but only if no allowance is provided for it. Settling, once understood, happens also to be one of the greatest strengths of a log building. The well-prepared or experienced log builder works along with the forces of gravity, employing it to good advantage ... thereby achieving an ever-tighter building as the decades roll by and the logs keep pressing evenly down.

Allow ample room to settle - ¾" per foot of log wall involved.

Doors and windows

Door and window frames can be made up on the job, and are often much more suited to a log building. Plank doors are solid and very serviceable. A three-batten door is made from four planks planed to 1-3/8" net thickness and 7½" width. Three 1½" battens are set 3/8" into the planks, glued and nailed to the inside. Such a door will not sag. However, shrinkage and warping could occur if the wood is not sufficiently seasoned. The use of cedar or fir is recommended.

Thermetically sealed double pane glass can be used as well as single glazed windows and may be placed solidly into a rabbeted window frame. The glass is bedded into caulking material and a ¼" margin left to avoid binding. Single sheets of glass 4 feet square were used in the house at Francois Lake and, with ample header space, have withstood many years of settling without damage. Sliding windows can be made by cutting a groove around the frame and placing two sheets of plate glass in the grooves in such a manner as to allow them to slide past each other. The top groove is cut deeply enough that the glass can be slid up into it, then dropped into the bottom slot without being released from the top. Ready-to-install factory-built windows which slide open, lock shut, and have sliding screens as well, have become extremely expensive. In this region such windows freeze shut (or open, as the case may be) in winter. So it seems better to install fixed windows -- that is, glass bedded in hand made frames -- and provide separate hinged openings for ventilation. This would be much less costly and much more efficient in use.

Gable ends

When the top of the walls are completed, the gable ends may be made using logs or framed with lumber or timbers. Hip or mansard roofs can eliminate the gable end but they are not commonly used on small buildings.

The gable end made of logs is held in place by purlins which are simply logs reaching the length of the building but lined up with the anticipated ridge. These logs will be lower than the roof line by about 4" to allow room for the rafters. Gable end logs may be pinned in place by boring two 2" auger holes through the log and the log below, then driving a 2" square peg into the hole. Purlins should be double-notched into the log below (see also NOTCHES OF ALL KINDS). This is different from the wall logs, but in this manner the ends of the gable logs will not be severed when the roof slope is cut. If the building is large enough to require several purlins, you will have to devise some means of getting them

plate) will have a ⅓ pitch. A roof having less than 1/5 pitch is not considered suitable for shakes.

Snap a plate line on the end wall of the building (see illustration). This line will be far enough below the top of the side wall to accommodate the expected rafter size. If vertical planking is substituted for rafters, the top of the side wall logs may be taken as the plate line.

Drive a small nail at the centre of the line. This will be directly below the ridge log. Drive additional nails below the purlin locations. Depending on the number of purlins to be used, the top of the first purlin will be located at ½, ⅓, etc., of the total rise. Don't worry about the void space between the top of the purlin centre line and the bottom of the rafter.

Select gable end logs which will produce very nearly this height of gable ends, less ½ the diameter of the purlin you have selected (each end will be different). Place the purlin directly above the measured location on the plate line,

then scribe it down to the exact predetermined height above the plate line. If the purlin is bowed, swing the bow up and in, until it is more nearly on a plane with the roof.

approximately in the right position to line up with the ridgepole. Following is a suggestion as to how this may be done, though you may find a way that suits you better.

We will assume that you are going to use log gables and that you are going to run the purlins parallel to the long side of the building. The pitch of a roof is arrived at by dividing the total height of the roof above the plate (called "rise") by the total span of the roof and expressing this as a fraction. A building 24 ft. wide with the tip of the roof 8 ft. above the top log of the wall (which we will take to be the

A very long building may require support for the purlins in the centre. This can be done with an extra log across the building placed one log below the top side wall log and perpendicular supports put under the purlins -- W braces can be devised if the span warrants them.

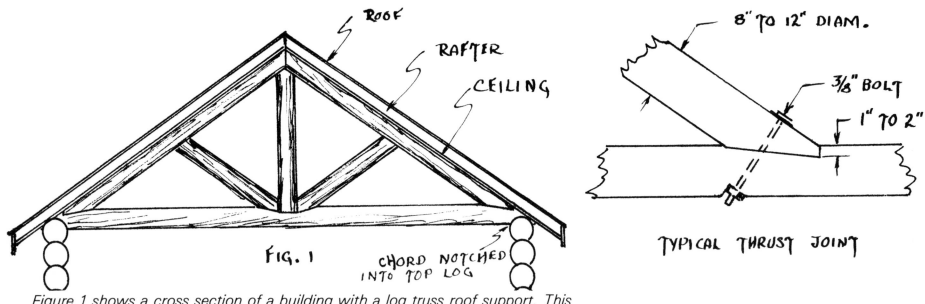

ROOF

RAFTER

CEILING

FIG. 1

CHORD NOTCHED INTO TOP LOG

8" TO 12" DIAM.

3/8" BOLT

1" TO 2"

TYPICAL THRUST JOINT

Figure 1 shows a cross section of a building with a log truss roof support. This truss could be built on the ground and used in the same manner as a nailed truss. Each truss would normally be placed 6 to 10 ft. apart. It has good appearance and strength.

The truss illustrated in Fig. 2 would be placed every 15 to 20 ft. It is tremendously strong and suited to larger buildings or heavy loading. Posts under each purlin may be used instead of diagonal truss members. The double chord members may be bolted together and a double ridge pole added.

RIDGE POLE

RAFTER

PURLIN

TRUSS

CHORD

FIG. 2

At left: Morley New nailing 2'' tongue and groove cedar decking on his home near Prince George. 2x6 planks on edge with fibreglass between were applied next, then 1x6 stripping, then hand split cedar shakes.

LOG GABLE ENDS

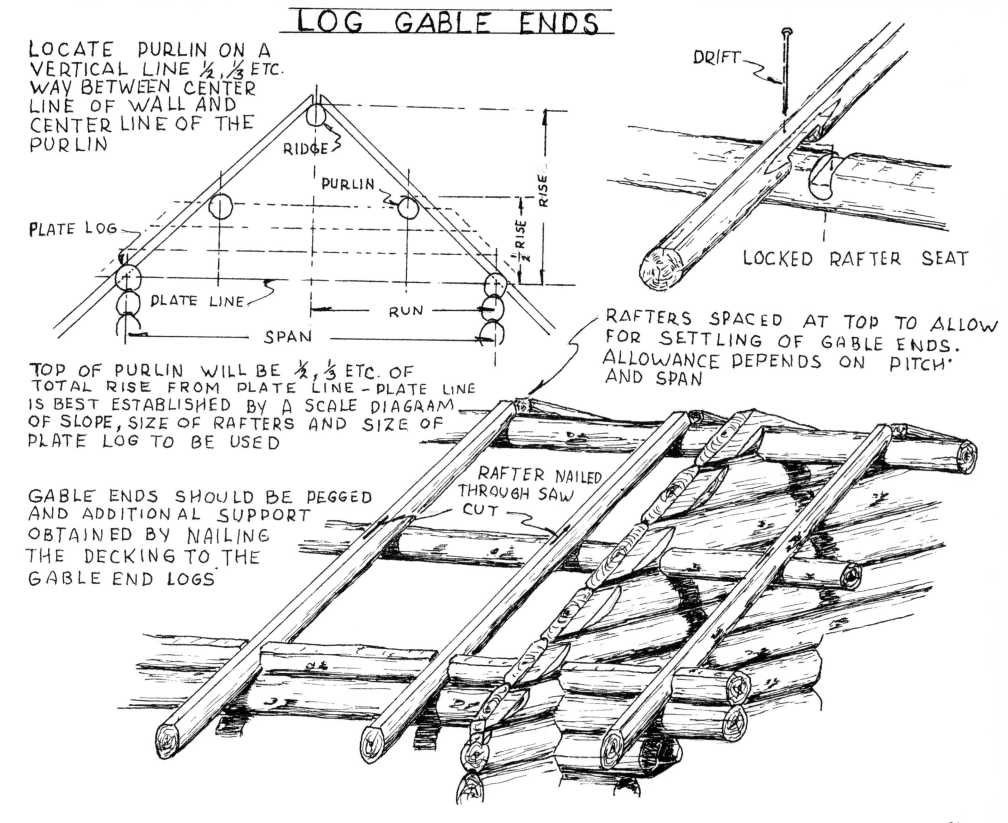

LOCATE PURLIN ON A VERTICAL LINE ½, ⅓ ETC. WAY BETWEEN CENTER LINE OF WALL AND CENTER LINE OF THE PURLIN

RIDGE

PURLIN

PLATE LOG

PLATE LINE

½ RISE

RISE

RISE

RUN

SPAN

TOP OF PURLIN WILL BE ½, ⅓ ETC. OF TOTAL RISE FROM PLATE LINE - PLATE LINE IS BEST ESTABLISHED BY A SCALE DIAGRAM OF SLOPE, SIZE OF RAFTERS AND SIZE OF PLATE LOG TO BE USED

GABLE ENDS SHOULD BE PEGGED AND ADDITIONAL SUPPORT OBTAINED BY NAILING THE DECKING TO THE GABLE END LOGS

DRIFT

LOCKED RAFTER SEAT

RAFTERS SPACED AT TOP TO ALLOW FOR SETTLING OF GABLE ENDS. ALLOWANCE DEPENDS ON PITCH AND SPAN

RAFTER NAILED THROUGH SAW CUT

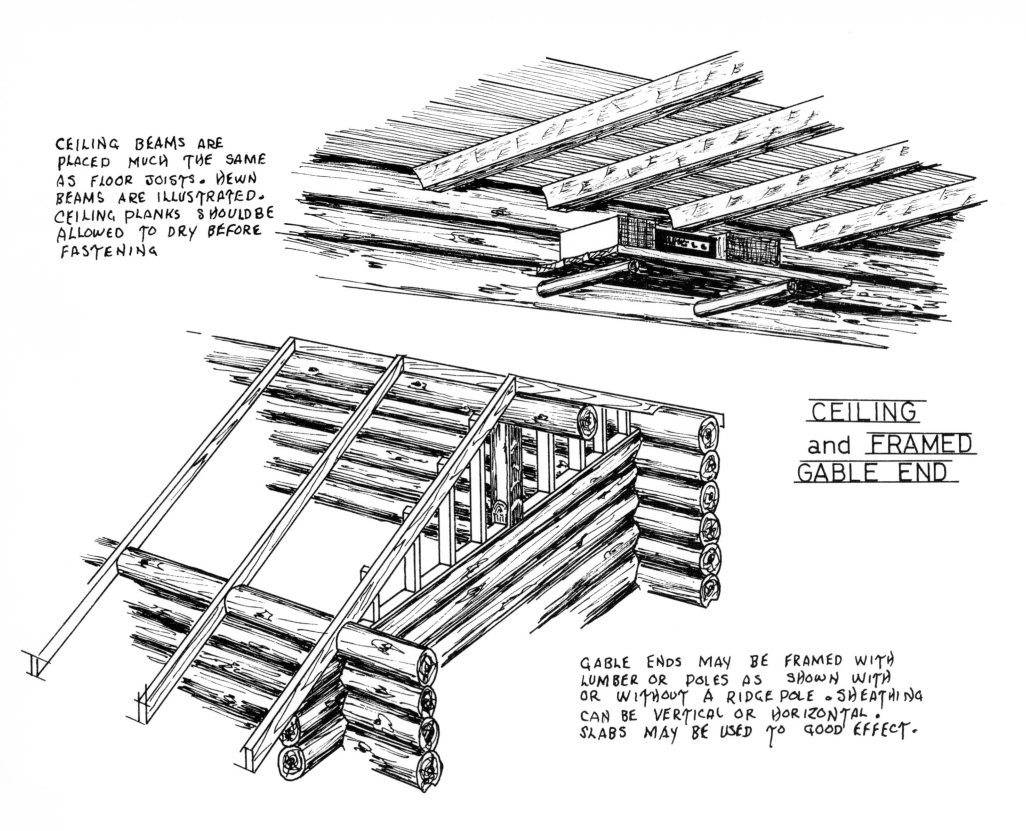

CEILING BEAMS ARE
PLACED MUCH THE SAME
AS FLOOR JOISTS. HEWN
BEAMS ARE ILLUSTRATED.
CEILING PLANKS SHOULD BE
ALLOWED TO DRY BEFORE
FASTENING

CEILING
and FRAMED
GABLE END

GABLE ENDS MAY BE FRAMED WITH
LUMBER OR POLES AS SHOWN WITH
OR WITHOUT A RIDGE POLE. SHEATHING
CAN BE VERTICAL OR HORIZONTAL.
SLABS MAY BE USED TO GOOD EFFECT.

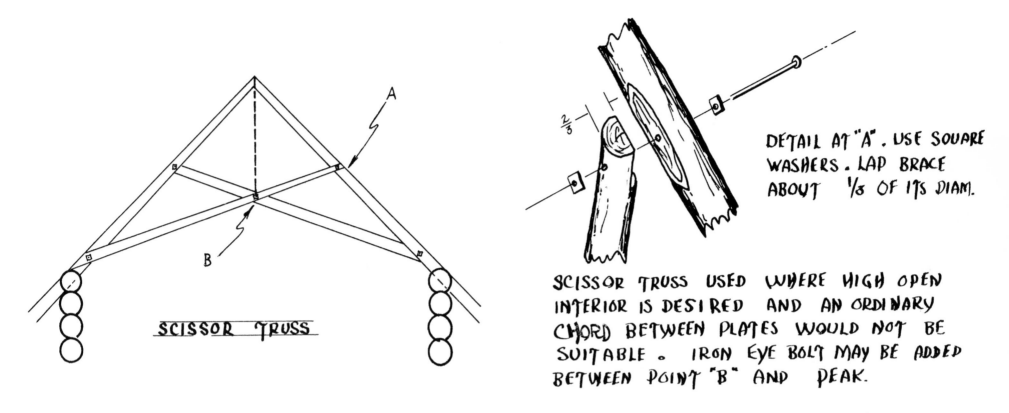

SCISSOR TRUSS

DETAIL AT "A". USE SQUARE WASHERS. LAP BRACE ABOUT ⅓ OF ITS DIAM.

SCISSOR TRUSS USED WHERE HIGH OPEN INTERIOR IS DESIRED AND AN ORDINARY CHORD BETWEEN PLATES WOULD NOT BE SUITABLE. IRON EYE BOLT MAY BE ADDED BETWEEN POINT "B" AND PEAK.

(See also LOG SPAN TABLES for Floor Joists, Beams, and Roof Support Systems by Mackie & Read, for log beam calculation and design.)

Rafters

Log rafters may be double-notched into the plate logs if they are small (see previous illustration) or they may be wedged into the plate log by cutting a slot slightly narrower at the bottom than the top. Rafters are then separated at the top to avoid hang up as the gable end logs settle. This space allowance should be ¾" for each foot of rise, if the gable end logs are green. Spacing at the ridge will not be required, however, if the gable ends are framed.

In order to align rafters or joists, position the members at each end first. Stretch a mason's line tightly between these and block the line up about 1". Now when a rafter is positioned in between these, it will be in line when it is 1" below the line. This method will prevent the accumulation of small errors, as might be the case if each rafter is lined up with the preceding one only.

Ceiling

Ceiling joists may be placed in a manner similar to floor joists. Square hewn ceiling joists give a good appearance. But consider carefully whether or not your plan requires a ceiling ... it may simply be hiding your carefully selected ridgepole.

Ceiling planks shrink excessively and, for this reason, should not be fastened down for about a year. If mineral wool batts are used for insulation, these can be removed, the vapour barrier removed, and the ceiling planks driven close together to tighten up the fitting. It would be well to leave a few extra pieces on top of the ceiling to insert into the space which the shrinkage will create.

Section through door

POSSIBLE LAYOUT FOR A ONE OR TWO STOREY BUILDING WHEN AN OPEN CEILING IS DESIRED. RAFTERS ARE SEATED AT THE PLATE & DRIFTED, THROUGH SLOTS, TO THE PURLINS. THE TWO TOP LOGS SHOULD BE PEGGED OR DRIFTED TOGETHER. DRILL HOLES FOR DRIFTS AND GREASE THEM TO AVOID HANGUPS.

VERTICAL POST IS ENTERED INTO LOG ABOVE & BELOW OPENINGS. OTHER FOUNDATION LAYOUTS CAN BE USED.

The walls of your house are now up and you will have put in a ceiling that can be insulated, or, if an open ceiling is more to your liking, the roof can be insulated.

It might well be emphasized here, the importance of good insulation. All your careful logwork could result in a cold and draughty house if cold and draught are, in fact, permitted to sneak in elsewhere. Care should be taken that ventilation is provided. Vapour barrier goes under the insulating material. Place a screened strip the full length of the eave as close as possible to the lower end. Strapping for shakes permits ventilation between the 2x4 spacers over the insulation.

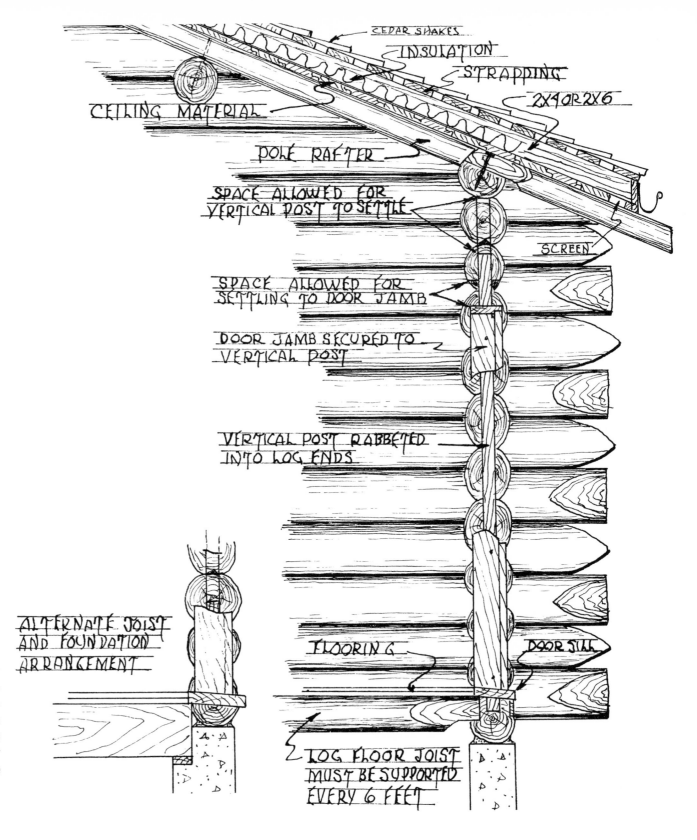

CEDAR SHAKES
INSULATION
STRAPPING
2X4 OR 2X6
CEILING MATERIAL
POLE RAFTER
SCREEN
SPACE ALLOWED FOR VERTICAL POST TO SETTLE
SPACE ALLOWED FOR SETTLING TO DOOR JAMB
DOOR JAMB SECURED TO VERTICAL POST
VERTICAL POST RABBETED INTO LOG ENDS
ALTERNATE JOIST AND FOUNDATION ARRANGEMENT
FLOORING
DOOR SILL
LOG FLOOR JOIST MUST BE SUPPORTED EVERY 6 FEET

Partitions

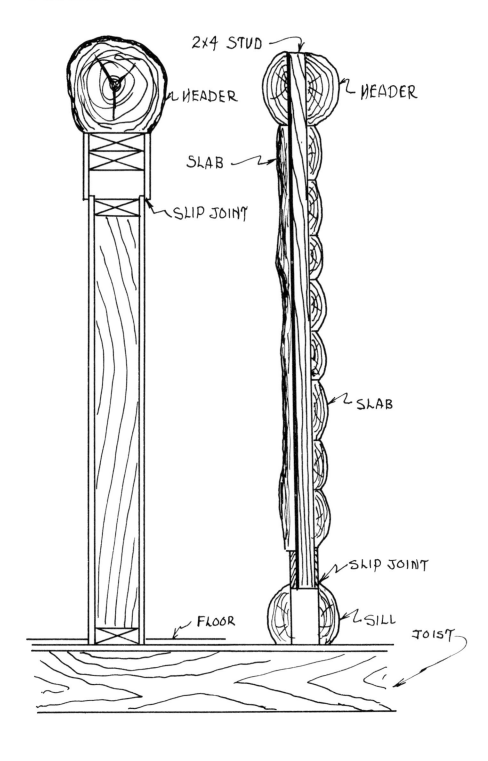

2X4 STUD

HEADER

HEADER

SLAB

SLIP JOINT

SLAB

SLIP JOINT

FLOOR

SILL

JOIST

Interior partitions, if they cannot be avoided, are best made of log. They are, of course, erected at the same time as the exterior walls are being put up. And interior partitions require the same average mean diameter logs as do the exterior walls, although many an architect or draughtman will specify that they should be made of a smaller dimension material. A moment's reflection will show that this is not possible, if interlocking members are planned (not, that is, without leaving large spaces between each interior partition log). Partitions should always be made to interlock -- i.e., to extend through the exterior wall -- as they provide tremendous strength and stability to the building in this simple way. This is of great importance when, as a general rule, no log wall should run more than 16 to 20 feet without some form of cross bracing. An interlocking log partition serves this purpose admirably. Log partitons also look better than a wall framed of other material. And if time is a factor, they require less work in the long run. It is well to remember, in the blueprint stage, that a log wall does take up a few inches more space than does a framed partition; but there are acoustical benefits built into that stout partition, too.

Log partitions are to be recommended in all cases, with the possible exception of a situation where either logs or space are in short supply. Even so, perhaps consider the use of a stone fireplace as a pleasing division of space, with the added advantage in certain houseplans of providing both chimney and backing for the kitchen stove. In our Southbank home, the only visible demarkation between the living room area and the dining-kitchen areas was simply where the rug changed to linoleum. We postponed filling in the bedroom dividers for several years because of the tremendous view of Francois Lake which, without partitions, could be seen from any corner of the house. As the family grew, we relented only to the point of putting up a bamboo curtain which could be lowered as needed, which was not often.

When framing partitions in a log house, care must be taken to allow space for the settling of the building. Partitions may be made to telescope at some place, or they can be made to fit a mortised recess in a header log. Whichever method is used, the main thing is to avoid the possibility of binding of the wall, a phenomenon which has been known to lift ceilings or upper storeys or to drive the partition into the floor.

Stairs

Stairs, too, must have ample space left to permit settling of the logs. A space allowance can be left at the bottom of the stringer, with the stringers mounted on wedges which can be shifted as needed.

Rough stairs and simple stairs are generally constructed on a sawn-out stair horse -- usually from a 2x10 or 2x12 but round logs can be used to good effect. Square hewn logs are also good.

A housed stringer is the best and strongest form of stair. Each tread and riser is rabbeted into the stringer. The groove is wider at the open end so that treads and risers can be wedged into place.

Stair layout is accomplished by taking into account the total rise and the total run available, or required, to obtain this rise. Easy stairs have a 6'' rise and an 8'' run. Steep stairs might have an 8'' rise

and an 8'' run. To place stairs in a total rise of 8 ft. with a riser of 6'' will require 16 risers and a minimum run of 15x8 = 120'' or 10 ft. Three feet is minimal for a landing, so the available space will have to be a total of 13 ft.

STAIRS

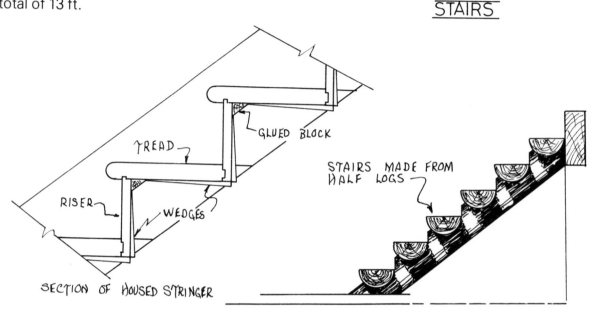

TREAD

GLUED BLOCK

RISER

WEDGES

SECTION OF HOUSED STRINGER

STAIRS MADE FROM HALF LOGS

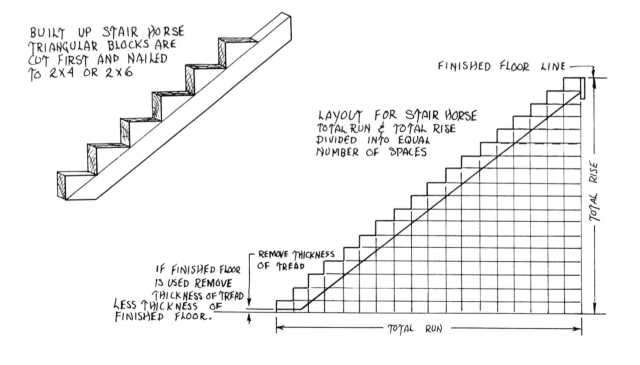

BUILT UP STAIR HORSE TRIANGULAR BLOCKS ARE CUT FIRST AND NAILED TO 2X4 OR 2X6

LAYOUT FOR STAIR HORSE TOTAL RUN & TOTAL RISE DIVIDED INTO EQUAL NUMBER OF SPACES

FINISHED FLOOR LINE

REMOVE THICKNESS OF TREAD

IF FINISHED FLOOR IS USED REMOVE THICKNESS OF TREAD LESS THICKNESS OF FINISHED FLOOR.

TOTAL RISE

TOTAL RUN

INTERSECTING WALLS

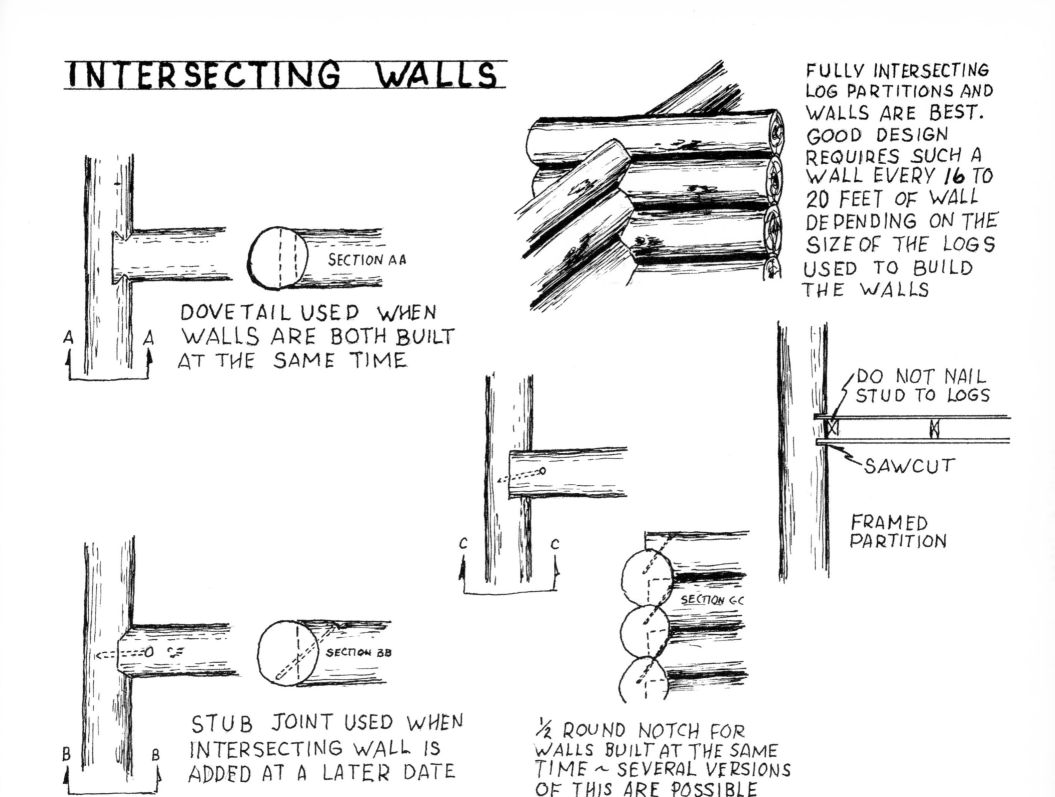

FULLY INTERSECTING LOG PARTITIONS AND WALLS ARE BEST. GOOD DESIGN REQUIRES SUCH A WALL EVERY 16 TO 20 FEET OF WALL DEPENDING ON THE SIZE OF THE LOGS USED TO BUILD THE WALLS

SECTION AA

DOVETAIL USED WHEN WALLS ARE BOTH BUILT AT THE SAME TIME

A   A

SECTION BB

STUB JOINT USED WHEN INTERSECTING WALL IS ADDED AT A LATER DATE

B   B

C   C

SECTION CC

½ ROUND NOTCH FOR WALLS BUILT AT THE SAME TIME ~ SEVERAL VERSIONS OF THIS ARE POSSIBLE

DO NOT NAIL STUD TO LOGS

SAWCUT

FRAMED PARTITION

Electrical wiring

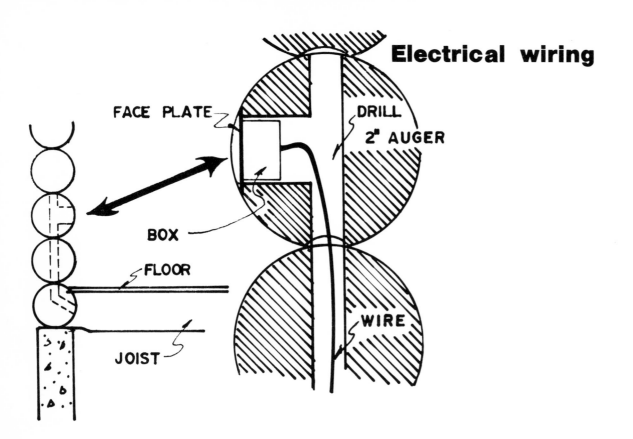

FACE PLATE

DRILL
2" AUGER

BOX

FLOOR

JOIST

WIRE

It is unfortunate when electrial wiring in a log building has the appearance of an added afterthought. Even in old, historic buildings specially made coverings for wires can be used to give an unobtrusive appearance. But in a new building, in which the total wiring layout has been fully planned in the blueprinting stage, such cosmetics are never necessary.

Recesses for outlet boxes are cut into a log at the desired height. The wires are pulled through the recess and carried either overhead or under the floor to the supply box. Auger holes should be drilled to accomplish this. Note, however, that the electrical inspector likes to see the wiring before it is covered or closed in.

A copy of the wiring code and much good advice can be obtained from the Electrical Inspector's office when you go to buy the permit needed to do your own wiring. Other books simplify matters a great deal for the layman, e.g., *Electrical Code Simplified for B.C.*, by P.S. Knight.

ALTERNATIVES

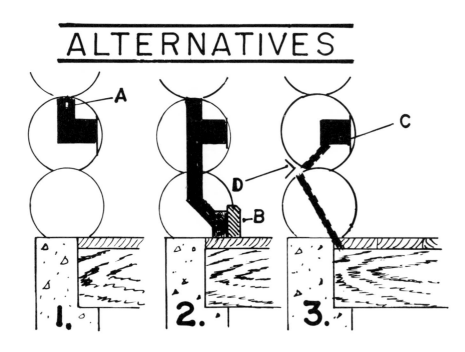

A

D

B

C

1. 2. 3.

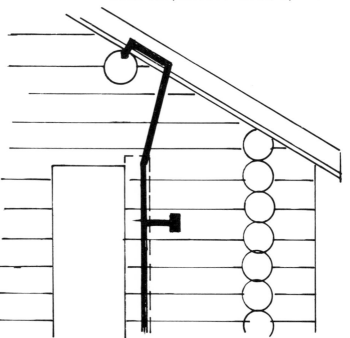

Shakes

Shakes are by far the most suitable roofing for a log building. They give the most appropriate appearance, are extremely durable and may be split on the site by the woodsman at little or no cost. With a proper chimney, they are no more of a fire hazard than any other roofing.

Western Red Cedar makes the best shakes but spruce, pine, fir, or balsam can also be used. Select a large tree with straight grain and clear wood. A large tree is the least likely to have knots at the butt, and it is true that the better the tree, the longer the shakes that can be split from it. So, saw the wood into the lengths that can be split most readily. Good shakes are 20 to 30" long, but are still useful if only 14 to 16" long. The rounds of wood are split into segments or bolts. Shakes should be split edge-grain off the bolt, the bolt turned end for end each time a shake is split off.

The tool used for this work is a froe -- a blade about 20" long, 3" wide and ¼" thick. A handle of 1-½" diameter and about the same length as the blade is secured to one end at right angles to the blade. The froe is driven partly into the cut with a hardwood mallet and the handle twisted to split off the shake. An outstanding effect can be produced by cutting very thick shakes (1-½") and having these sawn diagonally. The split side is then placed up and the material applied like shingles for an extremely rough-textured appearance.

Shakes are applied in double course runs, the first course being laid side by side not too close together so as to allow for swelling; the second course laid exactly atop but "breaking" (covering) the joins. The next course up is overlapped by about 2 or 3". They are nailed at both ends.

Shakes are especially suited to a steep roofed building with log gable ends. Courses can be run between each purlin and the dimensional change in the roof height due to settling is accommodated by the telescoping effect of the shakes. These, too, may be nailed at each end since the shift for each run is very little.

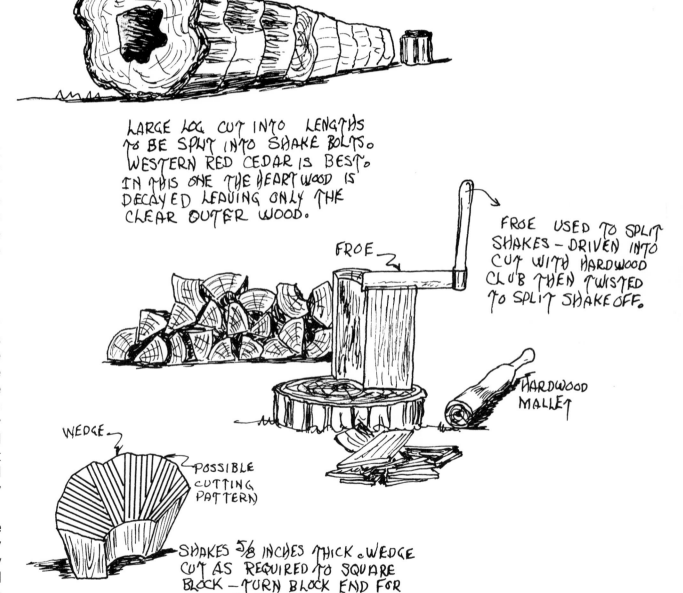

LARGE LOG CUT INTO LENGTHS TO BE SPLIT INTO SHAKE BOLTS. WESTERN RED CEDAR IS BEST. IN THIS ONE THE HEARTWOOD IS DECAYED LEAVING ONLY THE CLEAR OUTER WOOD.

FROE

FROE USED TO SPLIT SHAKES - DRIVEN INTO CUT WITH HARDWOOD CLUB THEN TWISTED TO SPLIT SHAKE OFF.

HARDWOOD MALLET

WEDGE

POSSIBLE CUTTING PATTERN

SHAKES ⅝ INCHES THICK. WEDGE CUT AS REQUIRED TO SQUARE BLOCK - TURN BLOCK END FOR END EACH CUT TO ASSIST TAPER.

SHAKES

STEEP ROOF WITH LOG GABLE USING PURLINS AND SHAKES. DIMENSIONAL CHANGE OCCASIONED BY SHRINKAGE & SETTLING IS TAKEN CARE OF BY TELESCOPING EFFECT.

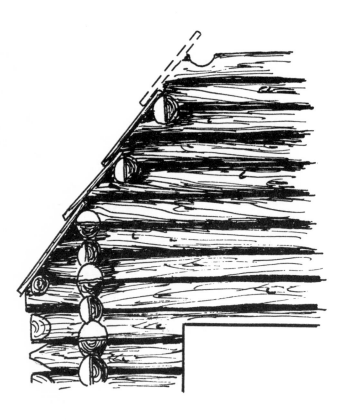

SHAKES MAY BE DIFFERENT LENGTHS OR THICKNESS AS REQUIRED FOR SPECIFIC PURPOSES BUT ARE GENERALLY 5/8 THICK AND 20-30 INCHES LONG

Fireplaces

Such great variety is possible in the exterior design of fireplaces that each builder will want to give much thought to what may well turn out to be a family focal point. My feeling is that a fireplace in a log house is nearly as essential as the roof. Not only does it burn the chips occasioned by the construction, but it also supplies a surprising amount of heat. The open flame seems to satisfy some basic human need derived, perhaps, from the security of the open fire burning at the entrance of the ancestral cave. For good reasons, then, let the material and design be a matter of your own careful choice. Linger over this part of your house plan.

But the building of the functioning interior regions of the fireplace is a different matter. The need for an open fire may be inherited but chances are that the know-how was not. A skilled stonemason can build any style of fireplace and it will send the smoke up and the heat out. The amateur mason must study some basic rules, too, if he is to acquire the knack -- and avoid the possibility of the heat going up and the smoke coming out and the masonry coming down. Perhaps the best advice to the amateur mason is that he buy one of the sheet metal fireplace forms available from hardware stores. These are simply a lining around which the stonework is done and, as these usually have arrangements for air circulation, this increased efficiency will more than justify the cost. There are many instant fireplaces on the market, too. Most of them work quite well if the chimney is carried about 2 ft. above the roof line.

But if you have approached the log building project with the intention of

completing the fireplace yourself, be assured that if you have the ability to work with logs you are also going to be able to work with stone and mortar.

Pour a substantial base when the foundation is laid. This footing will be about 1 ft. wider all around than the proposed dimensions of the fireplace. If the ground is very soft, go deeper and wider. The following table is a guide for various soil conditions.

CLASS OF FOUNDATION	DRAINAGE		TYPE OF SOIL			
			ROCK	GRAVEL	SAND	CLAY
Good	Heated Basement		No limit	No limit	No limit	4 feet
Poor	Heated Basement		No limit	No limit	No limit	4 feet
Good	Not heated		No limit	No limit	Below frost	Below frost minimum 4 ft.
Poor	Not heated		No limit	Below frost	Below frost	Below frost minimum 4 ft.

A solid base is the prime requirement of a good fireplace. A raised hearth has some advantage in cutting down floor draught, but should be reinforced with steel. If the building has a basement, an ash drop door can be purchased and installed in the hollow fireplace base so that ashes are removed from the basement level, otherwise the ash drop door can be placed so that ash removal is done from the outside of the house.

A suitable mortar for masonry is (by volume) 1 part masonry cement and 2-¼ to 3 parts mortar sand in damp, loose condition; or is 1 part Portland cement (type II), ½ to 1-¼ parts hydrated lime and 4-½ to 6 parts mortar sand. Workability is obtained through proper grading of sand and thorough mixing. If work is to be done in hot, direct sunlight, some provision must be made to prevent rapid loss of water. Use a flue liner above the fireplace form and then it is only necessary to "stack" rock around the whole thing to get a workable fireplace.

If you are building the entire fireplace yourself, the following rules may serve as a guide:

1. Flue size depends on the size of fireplace opening. Minimum size is one-tenth of the area of the opening but never less than 8x12".

2. Front of the fireplace should be wider than the back and upper part of the back should tilt forward to meet the throat.

3. The vertical portion of the back should be about one-half of the height of the opening.

4. The back should be two-thirds of the opening width.

5. Build a smoke shelf to reduce back draught, this is formed by projecting the throat as far forward as possible.

6. Throat should be as wide and shallow as possible but contain the same area as the flue. Obtain a well-designed damper from the hardware supply.

7. The sides of the fireplace are drawn together above the throat to form the flue but the slope should not exceed 45°to the vertical.

8. The firebrick should be 2" thick and laid with fire clay mortar or high temperature cement.

9. The back and sides of the fireplace should be 7-½" thick for walls built of solid masonry or 12" thick when hollow masonry or stone.

Place the entire fireplace within the walls of the house when possible. The chimney will draw better if it is warm and this mass of warmed masonry provides a comfortable, stable heat storage to be useful inside the household.

Whether the chimney is inside or outside the walls, care must be taken that the walls do not hang up on the stonework. Frame the fireplace opening the same as a door or window opening, so that there is room at the top for the walls to settle. The chimney may be tied to the wall with crimped, galvanized metal tie straps that will expand or stretch if the wall settles. But the chimney should not depend on the wall for support.

Use flashing between the roof and the stonework and leave 2 or 3" space between the roof material and the chimney. Cap the chimney with a sloped concrete slab through which the flue liner should protrude 1".

For the first try at fireplace building, it might be better to choose square-faced rock rather than field stone. Rock can be cut and some people lay the rock out on the floor to a full scale outline in order to fit the desired pattern. By this means a particular colour pattern, even figures, can be incorporated in the face of the structure.

2 FIREPLACES

SCALE 3/8 = 1 FOOT

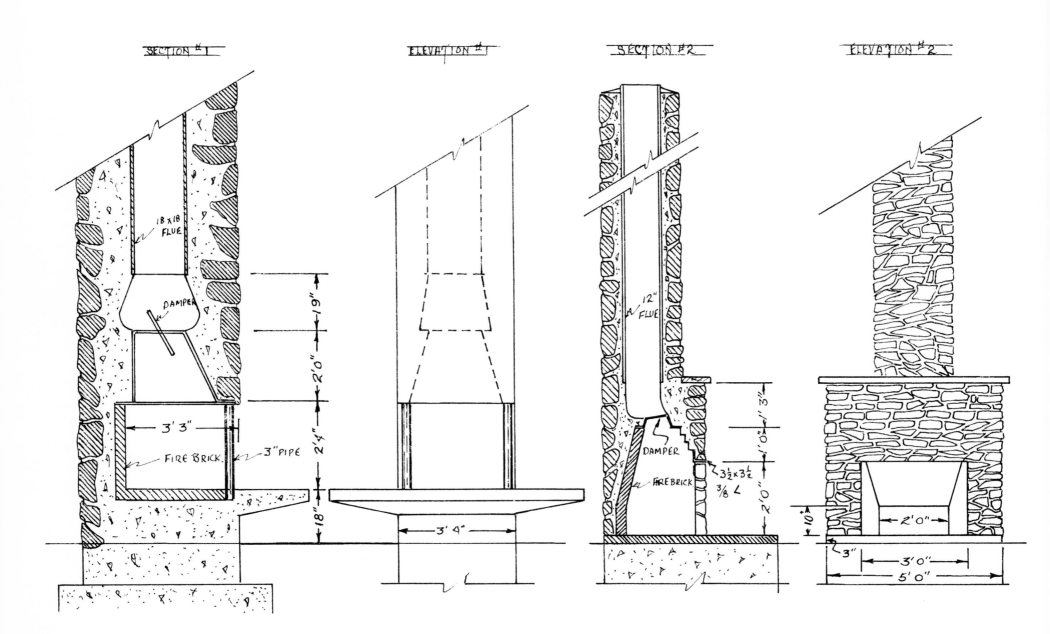

SECTION #1

18 x 18 FLUE

DAMPER

3' 3"

FIRE BRICK

3" PIPE

19"

20"

24"

18"

ELEVATION #1

3' 4"

SECTION #2

12" FLUE

DAMPER

FIREBRICK

3½ x 3½
3/8 L

3"

1' 0"

2' 0"

ELEVATION #2

2' 0"

10"

3"

3' 0"

5' 0"

The guest house

There is a great deal to recommend the small, separate house. Perhaps the most important point the student-builder should consider is the valuable experience it offers him, in preparation for a full-scale log house. On a small building, the logs will be a little easier to handle. If errors are made, these too will be smaller ones and easily corrected before the more serious construction project begins. So much can be learned from a first try that I'd recommend building even a doghouse except for the fact that no dog of my acquaintance would inhabit such a solitary and unheated edifice. Even the most experienced log builder can often be heard to say how he'd like to build another house (and another, and another ..) in order to apply the insight gained on every building. But this is never more true than on the first house.

There is also the economy of a small separate house, if it enables the family to move into a debt-free home for the first year. Some builders rent a mobile home or camper so they can move onto the site to work, but this can run to a surprising amount of time as well as expense to shop for, move, prepare a site for, and hook up this kind of mobile shelter and afterward nothing is left but a bare scar on your land and a debit in your savings. So even a speedy and none too painstaking job of building a cottage will leave something to be enjoyed later as a permanent improvement to the property. It becomes, for you, a truly historic site where your estate began.

A teenager can find, in such a cottage, the beginnings of independence. Midnight oil, trumpet practice, and bad housekeeping become almost unnoticed if the youngster isn't obliged to be too close to the family at all times. I think many a young person would return home, in later years, if he could remain his own boss in his own former hideaway.

Guests also feel much more free and comfortable in a separate cottage where their comings and goings cannot disturb their hosts.

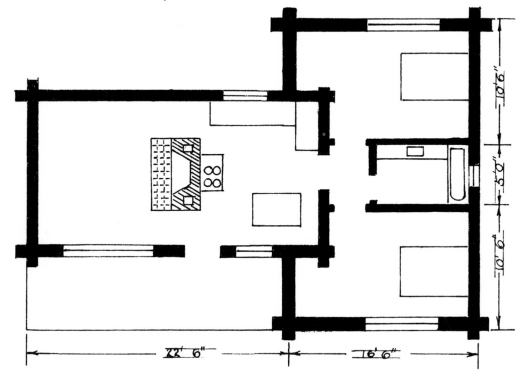

FRONT ELEVATION

Finishing up

It's a big job. Probably one-third of the entire project should be allotted to the details of finish work ... and what dividends it pays! The trouble with a log house is that it looks so good even half finished that sometimes people fail to realize what is lost by not completing the job. Also, the family is tired. They're impatient to get moved in. Plus the Lawg Caybun concept is never harder at work, doing its mischief, than at this juncture.

Carefully finished, even the plainest of log buildings takes on a rich glow of distinction. So apply the bargeboards and

fascia boards. Paint them (mine are a flat black) while you are up there. Install the soffits even though it's a miserable job or, trim rafter ends. Using a chisel or small plane, bevel ever so subtly a neat edge around the saw-cut ends of logs at window and door openings. Some interior log ends, especially those in plain view, might be lightly scalloped ... just enough to smooth away the raw edges, but with an artist's flourish. Such log ends in some of the ancient Norwegian homes would have been given a fully carved face. Suffice to say that everything done in detailed (not necessarily complicated) finishing repays a hundred times over.

The trimming of the exterior log ends can add a tremendous flair to the log home ... if well done. But use the utmost caution. It could be heartbreaking to saw deep into those months of hard work only to realize, too late, that too much has been cut off. I recommend an evening back at the drawing board ... and this is true even if you've planned this in the original blueprint ... as you may have a different feeling about the house or about some of the individual logs or about the way the house sits on the landscape in the reality. So sketch the house to exact scale and begin to trim the log ends, also to

exact scale, in the various possibilities. Avoid striving too hard after artiness which can so often drop a person into the trap of cuteness. A log home is honest, dignified, solid ... try to decide which profile best complements those qualities, then draw it again from another side of the house. Remember that even on a simple rectangular building there will be 8 of these profiles, affecting all views of the house.

Fanning the logs outward to meet the eaves gives a blossoming effect, adding a graceful lightness to a building. Another school of thought favours the "buttress" profile, that is, fanning the profile outward at the bottom. I rather like the

appearance of this (buttresses are usually stone, however, applied a hundred years or so after a stone building is up, and is intended to receive lateral pressure and prevent the stone wall from crumbling ... hence it is out of place, somewhat dishonest as mere decoration) but I never use this profile myself. First, as I have indicated, it isn't appropriate. But more important, I would be afraid of those extended logs catching moisture unnecessarily, and deteriorating. My log-end profile is simply perpendicular, with perhaps the two top logs drawn out to meet the eaves. Of equal consideration to the profile itself, however, is how much log is left and how much cut away. Make the error, always on the side of leaving too much ... a mistake which can easily be corrected later, if need be. But cutting off too much leaves the house looking pinched and poor, just as a too-small roof does.

Before any cutting begins, of course, the profile is carefully marked on the entire wall, both sides. For the perpendicular cut, use the chalk line with

a weight on the bottom, and snap a perfect cutting line with that. By marking both sides of the logs, the possibility of the saw being slightly off centre is avoided. Stand back and have one last look at the profile as it shows up in chalk, to be sure that's how it will look best.

Finally, a word of caution that log ends should never be painted or otherwise sealed. They must be able to breathe. See page 2, The Tree as Building Material.

When trimming up door and window openings, use the same care as with the profile of the walls. The longer I study the subject, the less wood I cut away. Around my window openings all that I remove is that small angle of wood which would obstruct vision, and then I bevel off the edge of that. Timber speaks for itself, I feel, and requires no frilly framing or axetrim effects. If you follow this line of thought, that is, enquire into your own preference at all times, whatever you do will be pleasing, the result of thinking over the possibilities and taking the one that meets the test of approval. Far too much damage is done to logwork by blindly following precedent. A defective building practice can become a regional hallmark, as happened in the Yukon where virtually all log buildings follow the models left by the U.S. Army during World War II: they are sawn (at great trouble and expense) on three sides, producing a cold, defective building. A tiny model of a log building, offered for sale in a Whitehorse gift shop, was also sawn on three sides although, naturally, was handcrafted. So, in doing the door and window trim … as with all other aspects of the project … first decide what is the best possible way of doing the job.

79

frozen, use a spoke-shave (a small tool, available from hardware stores) to go lightly over the surfaces without cutting into the log itself. Catfaces should receive special care to lift off the pitchy soft bark without marring their delightful symbol. The tracery of bark beetles should be brushed clean but not removed as they add great interest. Never be tempted to smooth down irregularities; in fact, never let an axe, adze, plane, or any cutting instrument gouge through the surface of the log. That sort of smoothing is, in my opinion, scarring. Nature's handiwork provides a natural embellishment which children, especially, thoughtfully observe and think over.

Trimmed, the logs should be brushed down with a soft brush. They'll need a good wash, too, but first a thorough sweep-up is in order, as dust is the enemy during the next three jobs. To wash the logs, use soapy hot water. Many people are generous with the bleach (which does lighten the colour) but bleach is destructive so, unless misfortune has blackened or mildewed the wood, no more than a tablespoon of bleach to a pail of wash water is necessary. If scrubbing is indicated use the softest brush which will delve into the nooks and crannies; never use a wire brush. The walls, ridgepole, purlins, and all exposed logwork should be done. The appearance will be changing dramatically now. The wood colours and patterns will be heightened, and the excitement usually carries this work along at a fairly rapid pace, as this is an accurate preview of how the logs are going to look when the oiling and varnishing are done. After washing, let the wood dry well.

A little wood nourishment next (which,

Interior Walls. If moss was used as insulation between the logs, trim away any wisps that might be showing. Trim off any stubs of branches -- an adze might be used if there's an expert handy,

otherwise it might be better to use a chisel so as not to shear off surrounding surfaces. Remove bits of bark. If too much cambium was left on, as is usually the case when logs are peeled while perhaps, explains why I am uncomfortable about the bleach treatment): a coat of boiled linseed oil. An old-timer once told me it's a good thing to paint it on hot. He says the heated oil does a superior job of penetration. I have never tried it but there is a ring of good sense to his suggestion. The boiled linseed oil needs about a week to form a dry surface.

Finally, a coat of semigloss varnish. Briefly I adopted some of the newer plastic finishes, until some doubt was raised about flammability.

Exterior Walls: Doing the exterior walls is simpler. Again trim off all the excess bark and knots and wash the logs with soap and water. In many areas, this should be all the treatment necessary. Harsh preservatives have become more and more suspect in the past few years. They are a deadly poison and the less of it scattered around the better. Superficial applications of this material can do quite a bit toward preserving the exterior appearance of the logs, but if the house is not protected from the influences of the sun, rain, wind, and all the other conditions that enhance deterioration, it will not prevent decay and bacterial infection.

It is far better to cut the logs at the right time, to protect them from the climate before and after building, to design and site to obtain ventilation as a means of preserving the building, rather than to depend upon chemicals to cover those errors.

Lighting fixtures, plumbing, heating, hardware: Lighting fixtures are of course the owner's choice and since good taste is so largely a matter of personal opinion, I hesitate to offer judgment. The builder is faced with a vast selection of materials and designs and his choices will, in large part, be dictated by his pocket-book. I would like to suggest, however, that lighting fixtures can be made and, like everything else, one gains skills in the doing. I won't offer specific suggestions here except to say that I have seen excellent work done with wood, metal, plastic, and coloured glass.

Plumbing is no longer the simple matter of a water pipe running into the house and a larger pipe carrying wastes out of the house. The water pipe still comes into most houses in Canada at least, and thank God for that. But the moment approaches when we, as builders, must act as environmentalists to safeguard the water and the earth, if there is to be clean drinking water left for the future. I urge any builder or designer to do as much study on the plumbing and waste disposal systems of a proposed building, as they do on any of the other major considerations such as the roof support system, the site, or the size. Consider that water pipe from entrance to final exit. Consider heating some of it with solar warmth and circulating it through the household. Consider the re-use of the grey waters emerging from bathtubs, washing machines, and sinks. And, above all, consider eliminating the 5-gallon flush toilet. At the very least, the flush can be reduced in quantity. But there are many present-day alternatives to a flush toilet which include oil, vacuum, biological, and incinerating toilets as well as aerobic tanks, recycling systems, and centralized biogas plants. No excuse remains, particularly for log builders who have a heightened awareness of nature, to permit the continued pollution of the subsoils and public waterways by sewage. This is especially true when the alternative -- the composting of human wastes -- provides a valuable resource for earth-building and plant growth.

Having studied the new research, whatever your choices are, your next most important step is to plan these systems into the house in advance of its construction. This means every detail: have all the routing for vent pipes, drains, tanks, and water pipes organized in such a way that they will not be affected by the settling of the logwork, nor will they interfere with other useable spaces. The

vent stacks, for example, are essential for the escape of any poisonous or noxious gases which may be forced back up the drain pipes from a sewer system, a septic tank, or from a composting toilet. But too often they are forgotten in the basic plan. Check, too, on the local regulations which dictate pipe size, material, and quality, as well as slope, run length, and so on. These regulations change from time to time and the builder should consult his local inspection agency at the time of final planning.

Wherever possible, I try to frame a combined plumbing and electrical closet between the kitchen and bathroom, as shown below, although some house plans will not permit this.

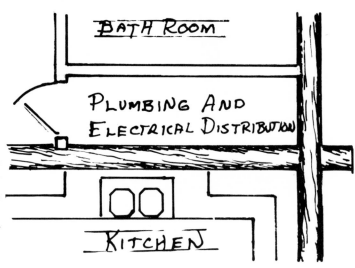

The best advice I can give to the builder or homeowner in regard to whatever he puts into his home is: let the owner of a log home be fully conscious of his proud possession. Let his sense of appreciation spill out in all that is done for the building from start to finish.

To plan the heating system for a building expected to last for centuries does mean the taking of a stern look at non-renewable fuels such as oil or natural gas. If after the year 2000 these fuels are still available at all, their cost will doubtless be beyond the budgets of ordinary householders. So I strongly recommend two basic approaches. One is solar heat, the source of which will be dependable as long as we can foresee, if we are careful. The principle of heat storage is particularly suited to the log building with its superior insulation qualities. Solar greenhouses on south walls will not only catch the sun's free heat but will also provide a natural humidity. With the state of this art in such an early phase of development, I hesitate to make further specific recommendations at this time; but I recommend a book called "30 Energy-Efficient Houses You Can Build" by an innovative architect named Alex Wade, if you want to get started right.

The other reliable long-term heating fuel is wood and I strongly recommend a wood-burning furnace and, wherever feasible, a wood-burning kitchen stove as well. This is not only for the cost savings, and not just for the comfort and good health of the occupants of the home. It is all those things and more: wood-fuelled heating may be the survival equipment of the future, when the brown-outs become the black-outs.

Not everyone knows how to make a quick fire in a wood stove for a summer's cup of tea, nor a long-lasting cool fire for the baking of Christmas fruit cakes. It takes only a little practice to learn this, though, and to be able to boil a kettle in just about the same length of time (from a cold start) as on an electric range. If the kitchen stove is in operation all day, of course, the kettle is always hot which means great savings in water-heating. Remember that hot water jackets can be installed in any good kitchen stove so that it heats a water tank for bathing, laundering, and kitchen sink. Then there are the long-baking and sweet-smelling dishes which can be cooked, at no cost: stew, bread, baked beans. Many indeed are the subtle ways in which people can work in harmony with nature and I think that none is more satisfying than the use of a wood-burning kitchen stove to prepare food. I note, over the years, that my wife abandons the double-oven electric range whenever a large group of guests come to our home; she claims that only the wood-burning kitchen stove can do top quality cooking in large quantities.

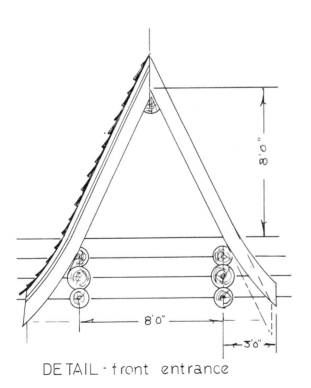

DETAIL·front entrance

There are excellent wood-fuelled furnaces being fabricated these days, readily available for purchase. Shop around for the best weight, temperature control, and size of firebox. Choose the appropriate size of heating unit. It's a temptation to try and get by with a smaller, cheaper model; but if too small a

heater or furnace is expected to warm too large a space, there is a serious fire hazard involved as the unit overworks. Buy big. Even if a big furnace costs more, you'll soon recover the cost in both the free fuel and in increased fire protection.

Fireplaces can also be made much more efficient, quite capable of providing back-up heat, by the inclusion of ductwork and forced air. If fresh air is supplied from the outside in this way, both for combustion and for hot air circulation, a slight positive pressure is maintained in the house and it does three important things: it provides consistently fresh interior air; it prevents minor draughts from being pulled into the house around doors and windows; and it prevents the reversal of exhaust gases from fireplace, furnace, or plumbing. Many people, otherwise, have to open a window in order to get their fireplaces to operate properly. This fresh air supply to the fireplace can be either gravity-fed or force-fed.

One final item: the debate about R-values is largely a debate about and among mortgage lenders. If seeking a CM&HC mortgage, for example, remember that they are concerned with the cash costs of heating with fossil fuels such as oil or gas. According to a CM&HC regional manager, you may side step the problem if you have installed a fireplace capable of heating some, or all, of the household. So this may be an added bonus.

Hardware is to a log building what a sunset is to a day; it may not be strictly necessary but it's an embellishment vastly enjoyed by all who see it. Hinges, door latches, and railings can be made to order

by specialty shops or the builder can make his own.

A head is an example of a door hinge which I do admire. It adorns a door on the centre block of the House of Commons in Ottawa. Like the sunset, it need not have been as ornate, perhaps. But in tracing out delicate bits of our heritage, the artisan has subtly built a hinge which, although immensely strong, we see primarily as a work of art. That's class. The kind of hardware which belongs on a solid timber building. The fact that the blacksmith is not as rare a bird today as he was 10 years ago is also a tribute to the healthy new log building industry.

Finishing touches

Everything I have described, up to this point, has been intended to help the builder create a home as solid and durable as a fortress. I have hoped that the builder would question all stereotypes, all frills and cuteness unbecoming to a permanent residence of superior construction. I have hoped he would discard from his houseplan any door, partition, trim, ornament, or object which could not account for its presence in terms of convenience, comfort, or structural necessity. For beauty in a home is inherent in the construction: its strength and stoutness and spaciousness. It isn't something that can be added later. But there is a time for a touch of drama to underline what hard work has achieved.

I am invariably surprised by the sudden blooming of even the plainest log building when the porch railings, for example, go into place. By this time, the chorus of praise and encouragement will have the builder wondering how he came to miss

trim. Diamond willow is ordinary willow that has been injured. perhaps by moose browsing, and later forms these patterns. Another wood considered to be ornamental is the burl, an abnormal growth occurring on the trunk of a tree. I have personally never been able to use burls. I find them as disturbing as any other kind of suffering and am uncomfortable in the display of a tree's deformity. To me, it is the smooth and healthy bend of wood, fitting perfectly to the grip of my hand and never freezing the skin as metal doorhandles do, that is a satisfying ornament. Or a stout curve that forms a knee brace. I have an 8-foot log of 12" diameter, curved to form the arch above a balcony doorway in my home and that tree is a special joy to me. The log builder knows the pleasure of an artist when he finds such timber in nature, the size and shape he needs to create a work of art. There is a story I like, concerning a log builder living in the Langely area of British Columbia. He'd seen many a tree, having been building with logs for 50 years. But on this occasion, he had been offered a 2-acre stand of old growth Douglas Fir which, having grown on level ground under ideal conditions were as straight as

harnessing such enthusiasm to a peeling spud months before. Straight young poles will form the bases of most railings and small trusses but there are forked and kinky parts of trees which lend themselves to special needs. Be guided always by a feeling of respect for the tree as a living thing, and simply acknowledge that in providing exactly the right fork or curve, that tree is a uniqueness deserving to be preserved and fitted as carefully as possible. One lovely example of this is an altar rail in the log church at the St. Laurent mission of Notre Dame de Lourdes near Batoche, Saskatchewan. As shown at right the altar rail had been formed by preserving the root crown of each tree to serve as footings for the

posts. Curved limbs were used as braces for the belfry in this church, and short lengths of matched poles framed an archway. The builder's feeling of reverence is clearly reflected in this work.

An ornamental wood, highly prized, is diamond willow, shown right as window

arrows, of a uniform 14" diameter, with only a few branches at the tops. When the old log builder saw these trees in all their perfection, he ran from one to the other, throwing his arms around them hugging them for joy. This, I understand.

As this story suggests, the life of the log builder has many satisfactions. In this discussion, we have been largely considering the personal satisfactions. But as a trade, it has much to recommend it.

It is impossible to imagine a more flexible, wide-ranging, or independent line of work than that of building with logs. Once the builder has created an admirable log house, his name belongs to

that project and he becomes known by it. Requests for his work will follow him as surely as night follows day, so he need never worry about where his next job is coming from. The log builder can set his own timetable so as to be free when he needs to be. Best of all, when he works he is not merely a cog in a corporate machine plodding mindlessly toward a more polluted planet. Instead, the log builder creates with his own hands a tremendous work of art, a thing of great value, in the conserver style. His landscape wherever he moved and worked, is now a better place. These satisfactions are rewards in themselves ... but the money isn't bad either. In this regard I have two concerns: that the

builders pay attention to their accounting and costing systems so that they set their prices to a level in keeping with other trades. And that the builders join forces, keeping as aware and alert of market conditions as possible, and setting their own strategies to compete in the market-place -- not with each other, but with the general economic steamrollers of life. If they learn to do this, in gentlemanly fashion, they will have safely reached professional status. My hopes are with them.

My own experience is that the supply of log builders has not, even yet, begun to keep up with the demand. For example, in the 4 weeks following the "Canadian Homes" story on my work, my office handled 3,000 letters from enthusiastic readers. Log builder demonstrations at Home Shows bring upwards of 20,000 visitors in cities like Toronto. The B. Allan Mackie School of Log Building (which I founded in 1976 and which now operates independently under the direction of a non-profit Society) has trained 1,000 fulltime builders and an estimated 2,000 more work on a part-time basis. Yet I know of no log builder, with the exception of those who haven't yet gained experience, who are unemployed or looking for work. The best ones are booked 3 and 4 years into the future. Most of them have several houses lined up, at all times.

Log builder training, on the other hand, is still not too easy to find in many parts of the continent. I wonder if this, too, is part of its mystique: that to find proper instruction is just as personal a quest as is the acquisition of building logs, the making of the tools, the design of the home, and the search for the site. In the end, the emerging builder knows he has made a long, personal journey.

For a while, it looked as if the community colleges and adult education departments were responding to the outcry for help in learning how to build with logs. But industry frowned and now the schools are beating a hasty retreat. It tells us a good deal about the public education system and it haunts me that taxpayers can so trustingly finance such things as timber leases and expensive logging equipment, for example, without a hope of ever being able to use them constructively as in homebuilding. When I fully understood this, I resigned from college teaching. It was the beginning of better things. I discovered that ordinary citizens have an enormous capability for solving their own problems, given half a chance ... and so it's entirely due to a handful of concerned individuals who have organized all my cross-Canada teaching sessions, that I have been able to accommodate so many participants. I

have taught classes of up to 100 people, from Vancouver British Columbia to Kensington Prince Edward Island. These privately-organized courses operate with a dazzling efficiency, marked by a relaxed air of cheerful enthusiasm. If something is needed, somebody fetches it -- no Purchase Orders in triplicate, no Bursar's office, no meetings of the Council to weigh the matter. I have immensely enjoyed these courses for the insight they have given me into this wide, clean, splendid land, and the deep feelings we all share, from sea to sea, toward this subject of building a good home and a solid future.

Perhaps a book, like a house, needs a finishing touch. But the unending interest in log construction lies in the fact that the testing and experimenting are never finished. For example, the tool I made last spring is the result of an idea which has been in my mind for several years but hadn't had the time or opportunity to

fabricate it. Several times I had mentioned the idea to other people who had tried to fashion the tool but it was never quite the instrument I had visualized. Then one day I had time, the metal with which to form the blade and a welder. The tool materialized and I was pleased with it, finding that it worked very well, just as I had imagined, for me. But it remained to be tested with groups of people who would find it a totally unfamiliar thing, so I took it with me for teaching three short courses on the Atlantic coast. Participants in those courses were shown the tool, and many of them tried it out. They, too, were pleased. So I believe I can safely say, now, that we can use this hand-held tool to carve with accuracy and a surprising swiftness the lateral groove in the logs. It is a delight to be freed from the chain saw ... and for those who lack accuracy with an axe, this new instrument gives a builder improved capabilities for this work. I show it to you, below, and I have

these audio-visual aids, literally stepping into the picture themselves after seeing the techniques clearly illustrated on film. Copies of these slide kits are available for purchase, and I have been pleased that so many public libraries have obtained these so that the public may borrow them as needed.

I am working also, year by year, building up 16 mm. motion picture film documentaries of log construction. Like the textbooks and slide shows, these, too, are helpful in the classroom but they also serve a wider audience as a general introduction to the subject.

Older readers will note also that some of my earlier techniques have been refined or have developed in new ways, over the years. This, I believe, is a sign of

only to find a way to make a lot more of these gadgets ... and to find a suitable name for it. But as I started to say, it is because of continuing experimentation such as this, that no one can say the last word on log construction, much less tell it all in one book. So I do look forward to writing one last revision of this work one day, when I know that I have finally laid down my axe.

There is also totally new work in log construction. For example, the slide show presentations I prepared for group use, right from the early days of this teaching, refining the details by adding drawings-on-film, then adding synchronized sound, dubbing in music, and finally adding voice-over-sound commentary of instruction. The final form of these presentations is the result of continuous experimentation with class groups as we searched for better and clearer ways of showing how things are done. Now I find it remarkable how quickly novice participants can advance, with the help of

the continuing health within the profession. If ever we say we've learned all there is to know -- there the log builders' profession will stop, stagnate, and eventually will begin to slip backward. This happened in the 1930's and was aggravated by a tendency among some log buiders to keep all the skills a mystery, a trade secret. Because of the near-disaster this caused for log buildings, I firmly believe that we must not only continually experiment, share the information, test out better ways of achieving ever better standards, but that public instruction is also part of that process. The more people who know how a log home is built, the more people there are who want one. The teaching will, in the next generation, fall largely to many of my old students and I urge them, at all times, to share their expertise freely. It is to them that I dedicate this book.

I am especially pleased to be able to say that the Mackie School of Log Building now operates year-round on a full-time basis, under its own executive director. As a registered trade school and a non-profit society, it is owned and operated by the society, governed by a Board of Directors comprised largely of teachers. Students come from all parts of this continent, as well as from South America, Australia, and Europe, to date. As a sign of its vigorous independence, the Mackie School is developing on a new front, combining environmental studies into log construction studies.

But when I know, as someday I surely must, that I must put the final touch to my work for all time, my wish would be to know that I had helped Canadians to build the most Canadian of homes, on their own land, indebted to nobody, dependent upon no external supports ... in short, to inherit their birthright. To me, a most interesting feature of that territory on the South Saskatchewan River where the second rebellion occurred, is the wealth of century-old log homes, echoes of those at Red River. Even though deserted, and built of crooked poplar, the skill and care of those log builders was such that the buildings still stand straight and true. Let their vision of a New Nation live on. Let the Canadian -- like the incomparable Metis of old, the buffalo, the trumpeter swan, the sea otter, and the tree -- put up some defences, most particularly from over-industrialization. Because an independent people in a clean landscape is a necessary basis if indeed young people are to have the right, if they so desire, to claim a portion of their native land and, on it, to build their homes . . . and to live at peace with nature.

A regular day of study at the B. Allan Mackie School of Log Building & Environmental Centre near the city of Prince George, British Columbia, Canada.

B. ALLAN MACKIE SCHOOL OF LOG BUILDING

A registered Trade School operating independently as a Non-Profit Society

Enquiries should be directed to:

The Executive-Director
B. Allan Mackie School of Log Building & Environmental Centre
P.O. Box 1205
Prince George, British Columbia, V2L 4V3
Canada

LOG HOUSE PUBLISHING COMPANY LTD.

P.O. BOX 1205 PRINCE GEORGE, BRITISH COLUMBIA, CANADA V2L 4V3

Current booklist

BUILDING WITH LOGS, 7th edition, by B. Allan Mackie

NOTCHES OF ALL KINDS, A Book of Timber Joinery
by B. Allan Mackie. The advanced text, profusely
illustrated. In hardcover only.

LOG HOUSE PLANS by B. Allan Mackie. Full blueprint
layout for 37 log homes. Readers may copy their
own blueprint directly from the book; or develop
their own, guided by the book; or they may order
a set of blueprints from the publishers.
Paperback only.

LOG SPAN TABLES by Mackie & Read. Data for calculation
of log sizes and designs for all log work, especially the
roof support systems. Small pocket-size booklet.

OPEN TIMBER ROOFS OF THE MIDDLE AGES by Brandon.
Beautiful facsimile reprint of an old English architectural
classic concerning the high skills of the mediaeval
English timber builders. Gold-embossed hardcover.

THE CANADIAN LOG HOUSE series, which started in 1974.
All back issues are available. Teaching articles, interviews
with practising builders, show homes, building
standards, reference reading, and more. Published
once a year on the first day of spring.

MACKIE SCHOOL OF LOG BUILDING NEWSLETTER
Employment directory, current news, listings of houses,
tools, etc. for sale. Mailed 6 times a year, subscription
by the year only.

Audio-visual teaching aids, by request.